19/4/99 (Book Token)

Creating Web pages
usin
C

GW01464090

By

David Weale

BERNARD BABANI (publishing) LTD
THE GRAMPIANS
SHEPHERDS BUSH ROAD
LONDON W6 7NF
ENGLAND

i

PLEASE NOTE

Although every care has been taken with the production of this book to ensure that any instructions or any of the other contents operate in a correct and safe manner, the Author and the Publishers do not accept any responsibility for any failure, damage or loss caused by following the said contents. The Author and Publisher do not take any responsibility for errors or omissions.

The Author and Publisher make no warranty or representation, either express or implied, with respect to the contents of this book, its quality, merchantability or fitness for a particular purpose.

The Author and Publisher will not be liable to the purchaser or to any other person or legal entity with respect to any liability, loss or damage (whether direct, indirect, special, incidental or consequential) caused or alleged to be caused directly or indirectly by this book.

The book is sold as is, without any warranty of any kind, either expressed or implied, respecting the contents, including but not limited to implied warranties regarding the book's quality, performance, correctness or fitness for any particular purpose.

No part of this book may be reproduced or copied by any means whatever without written permission of the publisher.

© 1998 BERNARD BABANI (publishing) LTD

Screen Shots reprinted with permission from Microsoft® Corporation
First Published - February 1998
British Library Cataloguing in Publication Data
A catalogue record for this book is available from the British Library

ISBN 0 85934 441X
Cover Design by Gregor Arthur
Cover Illustration by Adam Willis
Printed and bound in Great Britain by Cox & Wyman Ltd, Reading

ABOUT THE AUTHOR

David Weale is a Fellow of the Institute of Chartered Accountants and has worked in both private and public practice.

He lives in Somerset with his wife and three children.

DEDICATION

This book is for everyone who travels cyberspace, whether a beginner or a seasoned traveller and especially for those who value freedom of information in all media.

TRADEMARKS

Microsoft® Word, Microsoft® Excel, Microsoft® PowerPoint®, Microsoft® Access, Microsoft® Publisher and Microsoft® Internet Explorer are registered trademarks of Microsoft® Corporation.

All other trademarks are the registered and legally protected trademarks of the companies who make the products. There is no intent to use the trademarks generally and readers should investigate ownership of a trademark before using it for any purpose.

OTHER TITLES OF INTEREST

Contents

Introduction

This book has provided me with many hours of pleasure. I hope you will experience the same delight in learning how to create and design your own web pages.

This book covers the use of Microsoft® (Office) applications (Microsoft® Word, Microsoft® Excel, Microsoft® PowerPoint, Microsoft® Access, Microsoft® Publisher and Microsoft® Internet Explorer)

It helps you create web pages either for personal or business reasons. You can create web pages for use on the Internet or on a company Intranet.

This book is divided into sections.

- Common features
- Word
- Excel
- Access
- PowerPoint
- Publisher
- Coding (using HTML)
- Designing for the Web
- Putting your business on the Net
- Glossary

There is also an immense (and growing) amount of material available to you on the Internet itself about web design, HTML coding and so on.

Many of the techniques are the same or very similar within the Office applications and have therefore only been covered once within this book. You should use the **Contents** and **Index** pages as necessary.

Please note that the URL's (addresses of Internet sites) contained in this book were current when it was written, however the web changes day by day and some may have changed or disappeared.

Best wishes,

David Weale January 1998

Common Features

The Web Toolbar

The Web toolbar is common to the applications. The toolbar may look slightly different (with different program upgrades).

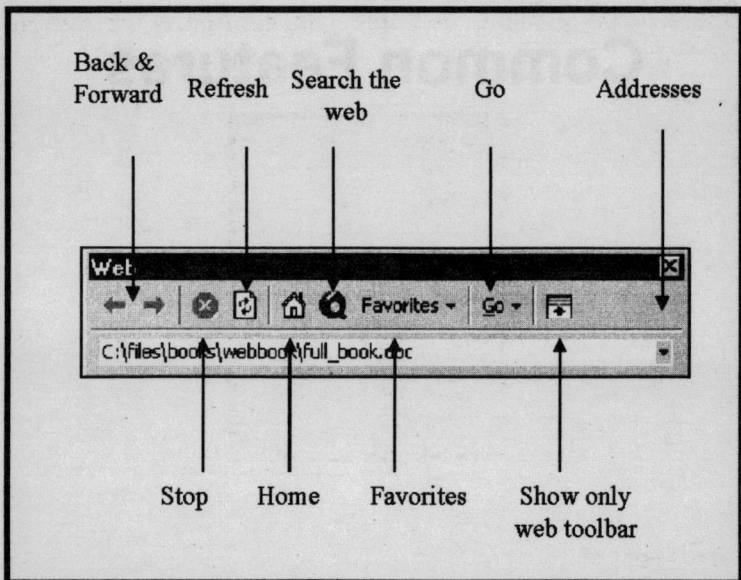

Back & Forward

These arrows move back to the previous web page you were looking at and (then) forward.

Refresh

This refreshes the page being shown (for example if changes have been made to the page).

Search the web

Loads your browser and allows you to surf the web.

Go

Pulls down a menu that lets you configure the various settings.

```
 Open...

 Back
 Forward

 Start Page
 Search the Web

 Set Start Page...
 Set Search Page...
```

Addresses

You can type in the address of a web site. In addition, clicking on the arrow to the right displays a list of addresses you have visited.

Stop

Stops the loading of the page you have selected, for example if it is taking too long or you made a mistake.

Home

Returns to your home page.

Favorites

A list of sites you have found of particular interest and have added to your (own) list of favorite sites. You can add sites using this button.

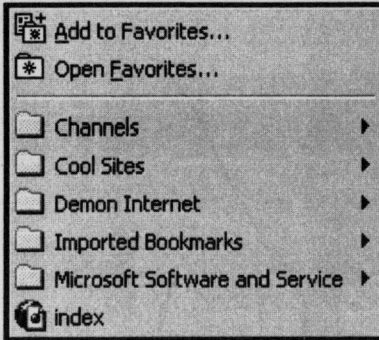

```
╔══════════════════════════════════════╗
║ 🔲 Add to Favorites...                ║
║ 🔲 Open Favorites...                  ║
║ ──────────────────────────────────── ║
║ 📁 Channels                         ▶ ║
║ 📁 Cool Sites                       ▶ ║
║ 📁 Demon Internet                   ▶ ║
║ 📁 Imported Bookmarks               ▶ ║
║ 📁 Microsoft Software and Service   ▶ ║
║ 🔲 index                              ║
╚══════════════════════════════════════╝
```

Show only web toolbar

This replaces the toolbars with the web specific buttons (to view any toolbar pull down the **View** menu and select **Toolbars**).

Customising your toolbars

The buttons and their arrangement will differ with the program version. If you want to add or remove individual buttons from your toolbars, pull down the **Tools** menu and select **Customise** followed by **Commands**.

> I suggest that you display the Web toolbar within all the Office programs

6

Web buttons

Standard toolbar

These buttons appear whatever type of document (depending upon your program version).

Insert hyperlink

To insert a hyperlink (clickable text or image) that enables you to jump to another page on the Internet.

Check links

This checks that the hyperlinks you have used within your web page actually exist. If they are incorrect, you will get the following message.

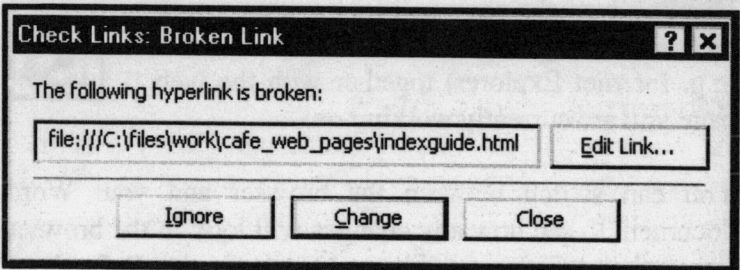

Check Links: Broken Link	? X

The following hyperlink is broken:

| file:///C:\files\work\cafe_web_pages\indexguide.html | Edit Link... |

| Ignore | Change | Close |

Web toolbar

To display the additional tools available within the web toolbar.

Background

To alter the colour of the page background (be careful to make sure that your page is easy to read by using a background that does not conflict with the text).

HTML documents

These buttons may appear when you have saved a file as an HTML type file (again depending upon your program version).

Form design

To begin the process of designing forms within your web page.

Web page preview

Displays how the page will look within a web browser. Using this button loads the browser (e.g. Internet Explorer) together with the web page you are currently working on.

You can switch between the browser and your Word document to see how any changes will look in the browser (remember to save the file and click on the **Refresh** or **Reload** button in the browser to see the changes).

Word

Creating a web page

You can create a web page in various ways; each will be described in turn.

Starting A New File

When you select **File**, **New** and then **Web Pages**, there are two buttons to help you create your masterpiece, **Web Page Wizard** and **Blank Web Wizard**

The others buttons are **More Cool Stuff** which enables you to download files from the Microsoft Internet site, **Conversion Wizard** which lets you convert several files from their original format into web page format and **What's New** which explains the new features).

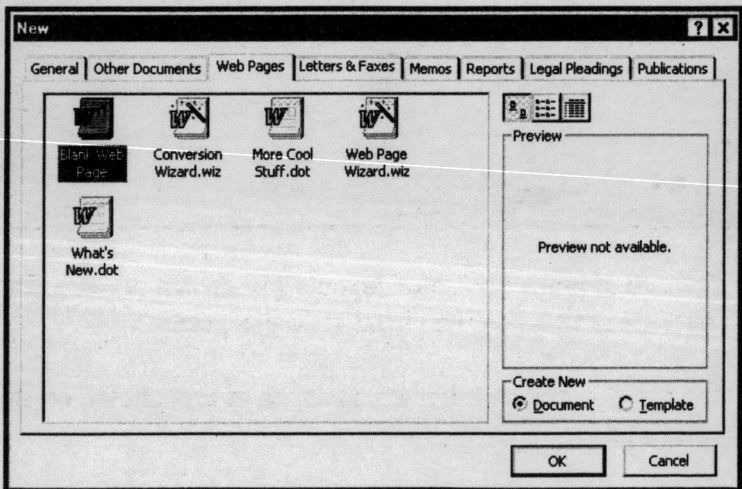

Web Page Wizard

This automates the procedure for creating a web page and is a good place to start your experiments.

Wizards are layouts for different types of web pages and the wizard takes you through various layouts, from which you make choices.

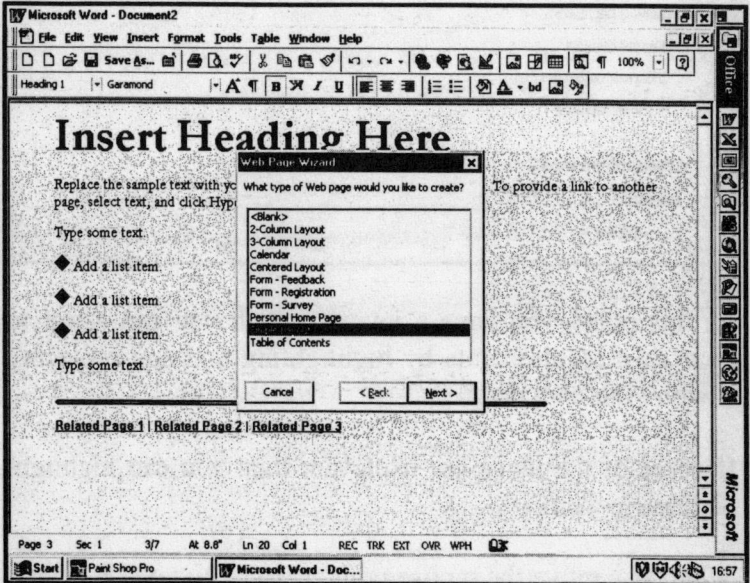

You are given a choice of layouts (as shown above). The next step is to select the visual style you prefer.

The result could be a home page such as that shown on the next page.

Insert Heading Here

Subheading

Contents

Work Information

Hot List

Contact Information

Current Projects

Biographical Information

Personal Interests

Work Information

Job title

Type some text

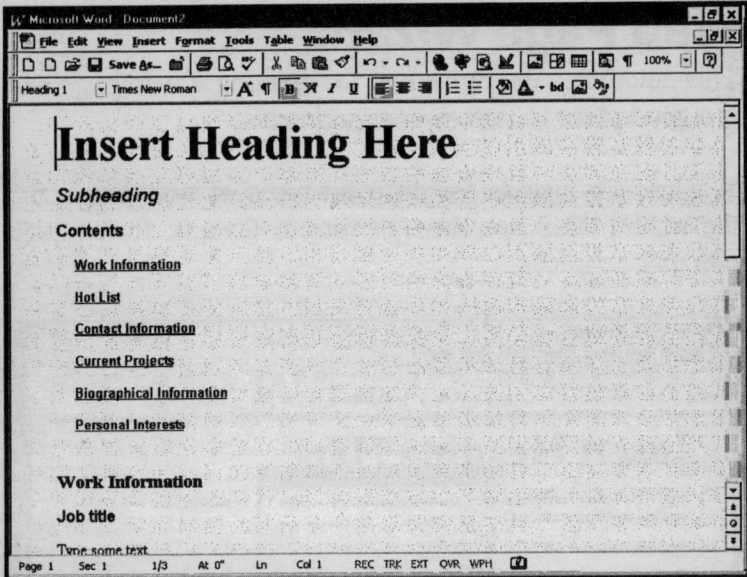

At this point, you have a layout, which you can adapt to your own requirements by highlighting text and replacing it with your own details.

If some of the items are irrelevant then you can highlight and delete them.

When you move the mouse pointer over any text or picture and a small hand appears, this is a **hypertext link** and by clicking you jump a new web page (or section within that page, although only some of the layouts use this technique).

The result after entering the text is shown opposite (viewed using Microsoft Explorer).

Remember that you can view the page in the browser by clicking on the **Web Page Preview** button. You will be prompted to save the file before viewing it in the browser.

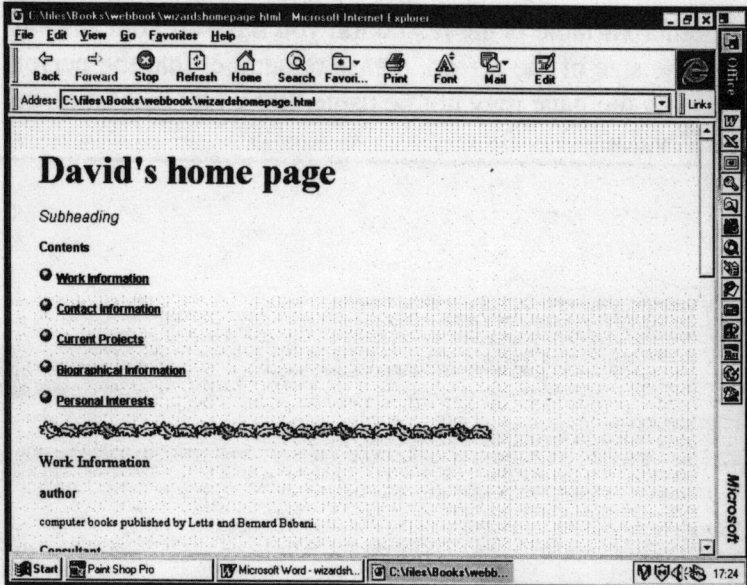

Using a browser

To see how the page will really look and how the **links** work, it is best to view the pages in a browser such as Microsoft Explorer; (you can use this off-line without incurring any telephone or ISP costs).

This is necessary, as the page may not look precisely the same within the Office program and the browser.

You should test your pages in as many browsers as possible so that you can ensure the greatest possible viewer satisfaction (nowadays this probably means Explorer and Netscape).

Another variable is the resolution you have on your display and the size of the screen, please remember that the person viewing the page may not be using 800 x 600 resolution on a 15" v.d.u.

Blank Web page

The other method of creating pages from the **File New** menu is the **Blank Web Page**.

As you can see, using this results in a blank screen upon which you can create your web page.

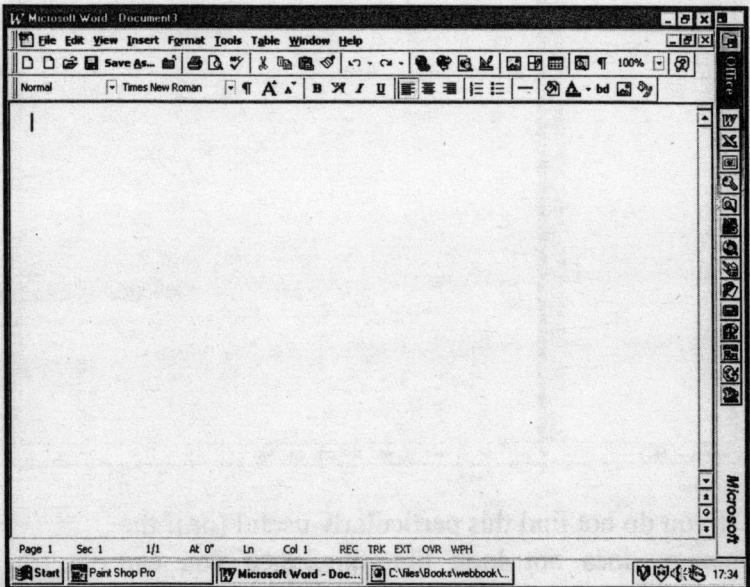

The file type will default to HTML when you save.

Online Layout

Pull down the **View** menu and select **Online Layout**. As you can see, the screen is split into two sections.

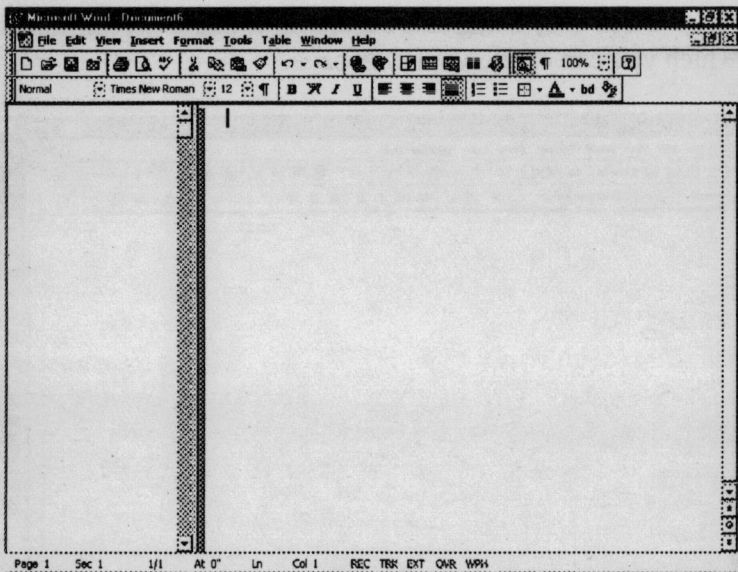

If you do not find this particularly useful (or if the screen does not look like this, then you can switch between full screen and this screen by clicking on the **Document Map** button). Now, construct your web page using the various text and graphic tools available.

Working with Word files

Another option is to create your page as a normal Word document and then save it as an HTML file. However, some features of Word are not supported by HTML.

You can also convert an existing Word file into HTML so that it becomes a web page by saving it as an HTML file.

This is quick but the results may not be as good as designing a web page properly.

Saving files

You must save the file as an **HTML** file and the **File** menu has a **Save as HTML** option. In addition, the **Save As** dialog box has the option **Save As Type**. If you scroll down to the bottom of the list there is the **HTML** type shown.

Working with web pages

Once you have saved a file as an **HTML** file, you will notice that many of the menus are slightly different. The reason for this is that some of the features of Word are not supported by the HTML language and will not work properly.

Working with the source code

If you are familiar with the HTML language then you can alter parts of the code itself.

To do this pull down the **View** menu and select **HTML Source**.

The screen will display the code and you can edit this and save the results, before returning to the original screen.

It really is worthwhile having an understanding of **HTML** as it allows you to alter or adjust the look and feel of the page very effectively. There is an introduction to HTML coding later in the book.

Below is an example of the code (from a web page shown earlier).

```
Microsoft Word - index.html
File  Edit  View  Insert  Tools  Window  Help
Exit HTML Source  Save As...  100%

<HTML>
<HEAD>
<META HTTP-EQUIV="Content-Type" CONTENT="text/html; charset=windows-1252">
<META NAME="Generator" CONTENT="Microsoft Word 97">
<TITLE>index</TITLE>
<META       NAME="Template"        CONTENT="C:\Program       Files\Microsoft
Office\Templates\handouts.dot">
</HEAD>
<BODY LINK="#0000ff" VLINK="#800080">

<P> </P><IMG SRC="logo.gif" ALIGN="LEFT" HSPACE=12 WIDTH=118 HEIGHT=71>
<B><FONT FACE="Comic Sans MS" SIZE=7 COLOR="#008000"><P ALIGN="CENTER">Yeovil
College</P>
</B></FONT><FONT FACE="Arial" SIZE=6 COLOR="#ff0000"><P ALIGN="CENTER">Business
&amp; Technology</P>
</FONT><P ALIGN="JUSTIFY"><IMG SRC="line1.gif" WIDTH=546 HEIGHT=4></P>
<FONT SIZE=5><P ALIGN="RIGHT">Full-time courses 1997/98</P>
<P ALIGN="RIGHT"> </P>
<P> </P>
</FONT><P ALIGN="JUSTIFY"> </P>
<P ALIGN="JUSTIFY"> </P>
<P ALIGN="JUSTIFY"> </P>
<P ALIGN="JUSTIFY"> </P>
<P ALIGN="JUSTIFY"> </P></BODY>
</HTML>

Page 1   Sec 1      1/1    At 1"    Ln 1  Col 1    REC TRK EXT OVR WPH
```

The Source Toolbar

If you do alter the code, you should
save the file (you will be prompted
if you have not) and then return to
the original by clicking on the **Exit**
button.

Exit HTML Source

How to make your web page communicate

This section looks at the various tools and techniques you can use to make your web pages both attractive to look at and able to communicate with the reader effectively.

One of the major advantages of working with the Microsoft Office web tools is that you can use most of the commands and techniques in the same way as you would if you were producing a non-web page.

Although not all of the features of the programs are available for creating web pages, most are, and you can use many of the multi-media techniques as well (for example you can add sound or movie clips to your page).

Be **very** careful if you decide to add sound or visuals to your page as they are demanding on system resources, both yours and the person downloading your pages.

Remember that most people downloading your pages may not have the very latest technology and may be working with slow modems and (even) text only browsers.

Working with a page

Before starting, you need to decide how you are going to build your pages.

One way is to enter all the text and pictures and then to format them.

Alternatively, you can format the text as you enter it, this has the advantage of enabling you to see the page as it is created.

Whichever method you choose, there are many simple techniques you can use to enhance your work.

Text Formatting

Format font

You can alter the size and type of font, make it bold, italic and so on (remember that there are also buttons for **bold**, *italic* and underline on the toolbar).

To alter any text you must highlight it.

The dialog box is shown for reference.

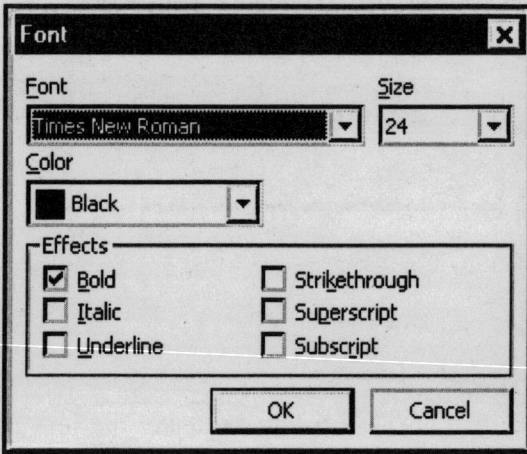

Note the font size buttons on the toolbar, these enable you to make the (highlighted) text a size bigger or smaller, and you can repeat this until you reach the maximum or minimum size.

You can also use these buttons to alter the size of the text pointer, before entering the text, so that the text that is (then) typed is correspondingly altered.

Text case

For those of us who type without always looking at the screen, there is a **Change Case** command. This is found in the **Format** menu and can save an enormous amount of time and frustration.

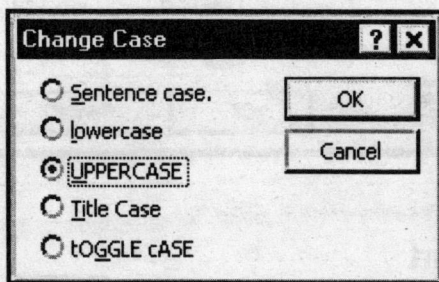

Change Case	?	X

○ Sentence case.
○ lowercase
⊙ UPPERCASE
○ Title Case
○ tOGGLE cASE

OK
Cancel

You can also use the **Shift** and **F3** buttons to similar effect.

Text colour

You can change the text colour by using the text colour button. If you click on the button, the text will alter to the colour shown.

If you want to alter it to another colour simply click on the arrow to the right of the button and there is a display of the colours available.

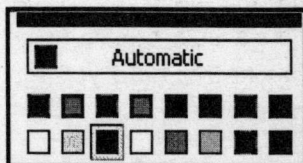

Automatic

If you pull down the **Format** menu and then select **Text Colour**, you can alter the colour of **Hyperlinks** and **Followed hyperlinks** (a followed hyperlink means that you have actually clicked on that hyperlink and gone to the page). However this may confuse the viewer who is used to the standard colours.

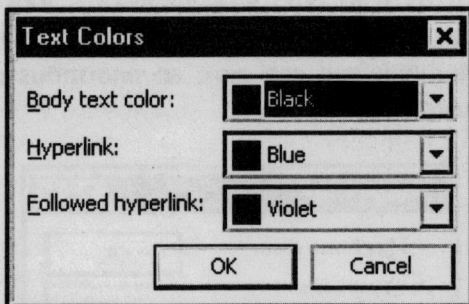

Text Colors	✕
Body text color:	Black ▾
Hyperlink:	Blue ▾
Followed hyperlink:	Violet ▾
	OK Cancel

Alignment
Similarly, you can align the text using the alignment buttons. Note that justification is not supported.

Text lists

You can create numbered or bulleted lists of text. To do this you may either:

☐ highlight the list and add bullets or numbers to it or

☐ you can begin a list with a bullet or number and then add to the list by using the **return** key to move onto the next item in the list. If you choose this method, you need to hit the **return** key twice to end the creation of bullets or numbers.

If you want more variety, try pulling down the **Format** menu and selecting **Bullets and Numbering**.

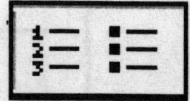

The dialog boxes are shown below, note that there is a **More** button within **Bullets**. You can use any (**.gif**) image as a bullet.

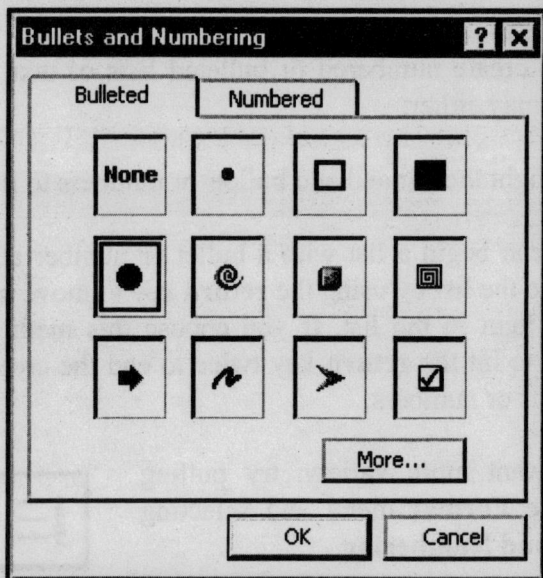

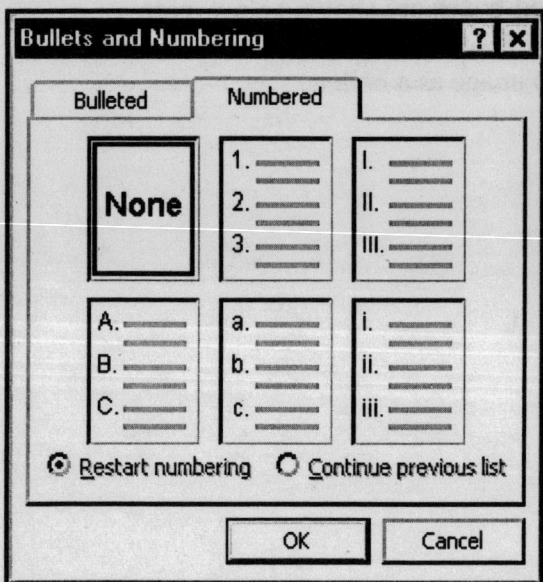

Here is an example of how bullets and numbering looks in the browser.

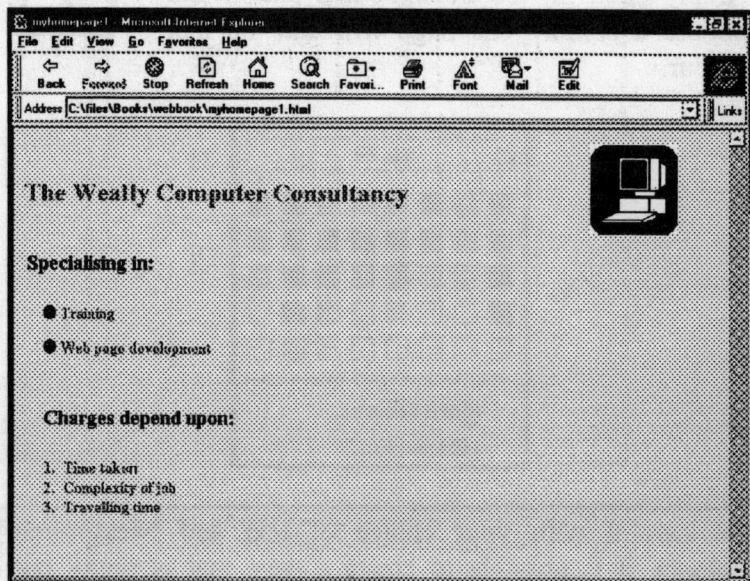

Background colours

Your page background can be of any colour, simply click on the **background** button and choose a colour. The page will take on that colour.

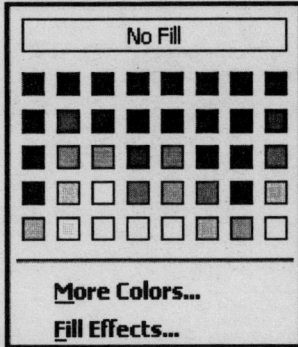

No Fill

More Colors...

Fill Effects...

Be careful with your choice of text and background colours, it is possible to create a page that is pretty but unreadable.

A coloured background may be easier for the viewer to read.

Try for a contrast between the text and the background, dark type on a light background or vice versa may work well.

You can also add **Fill Effects** to the page, these are textured backgrounds as opposed to a single colour.

Fill Effects

Texture

Texture:

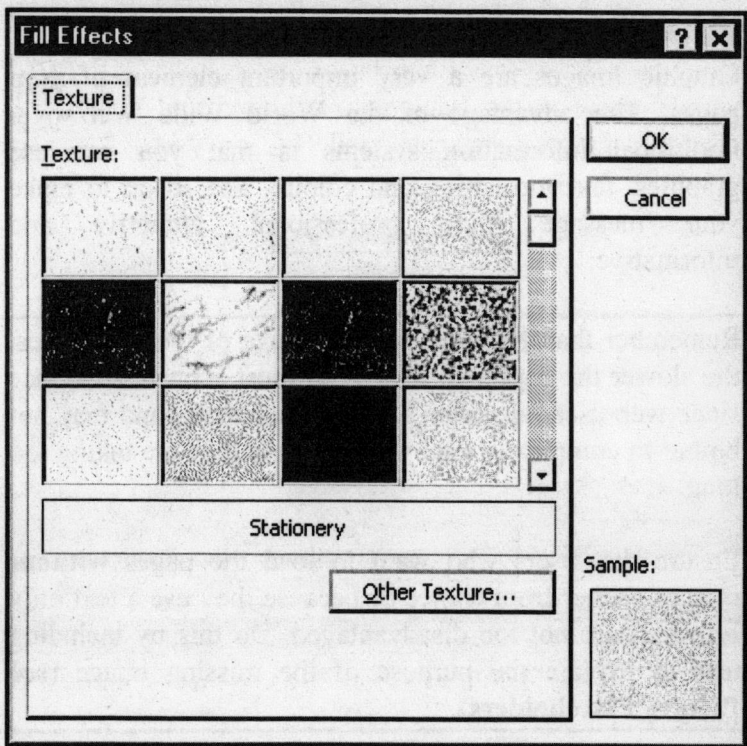

Stationery

Other Texture...

OK

Cancel

Sample:

Working with graphics

Graphic images are a very important element of your pages. The advantage of the World Wide Web over traditional information systems is that you can use graphics, text formatting and colours and so on to make your message more professional, attractive and informative.

Remember that the more use you make of the techniques, the slower the page will load. You must achieve a balance since web users are often impatient creatures and may not bother to completely load your pages if they are taking too long.

Ensure that users who want to load the pages **without** images (either from choice or because they use a text only browser) are not too disadvantaged. Do this by including text to explain the purpose of the missing image (see **Picture Placeholders**).

To insert a picture, click on the **Insert Picture** button and you will see the dialog box. Find the picture or other graphic you want to include and insert it.

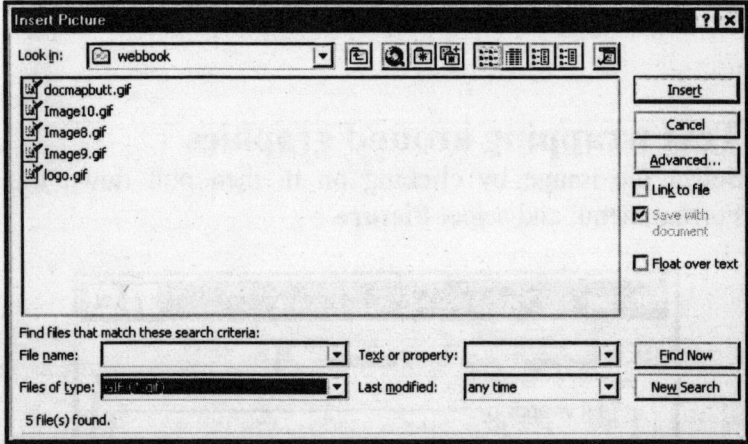

Insert Picture dialog box:

Look in: webbook

- docmapbutt.gif
- Image10.gif
- Image8.gif
- Image9.gif
- logo.gif

Insert
Cancel
Advanced...
☐ Link to file
☑ Save with document
☐ Float over text

Find files that match these search criteria:

File name:
Text or property:
Files of type: gif (*.gif)
Last modified: any time

Find Now
New Search

5 file(s) found.

Very Important

Web pages can only support a limited range of graphic file formats, the most popular are **GIF** and **JPEG**, both have advantages and disadvantages in terms of image quality and filesize (speed of download).

You may need a program to convert from other file formats to these. There are many available, e.g. Paint Shop Pro, Picture Publisher and so on.

Once the graphic has been inserted into the page, you can modify it in various ways.

Aligning graphics

Click on the graphic and you can use the **Centre**, **Left** and **Right** alignment buttons.

The default is to align to the left, with no text wrapping around the graphic.

Text wrapping around graphics

Select the image by clicking on it, then pull down the Format menu, and select **Picture**.

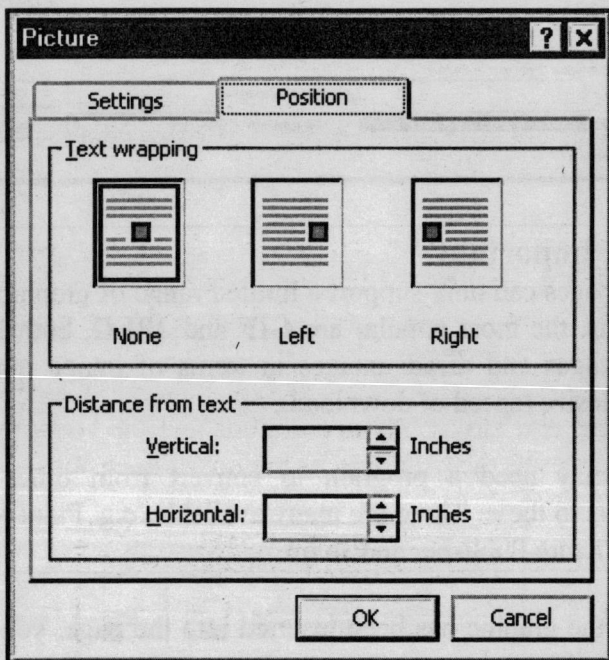

You can choose to wrap the text around the graphic to the left or right. You can also alter the distance from the graphic to the text by using the **Distance from text** measurements (either by typing them in or by using the arrows to the right of each measurement).

The program may revert to **None** (**text wrapping**) if you move or otherwise alter the image, this is something to be careful of and is irritating. You may also lose the right alignment of some graphic images when the file is converted into HTML.

Using the Picture toolbar

It is easier, if you are working with graphics, to use the **Picture** toolbar instead of having to use the pull down menus (it is quicker and less irritating).

To display the **Picture** toolbar, pull down the **View** menu and select **Toolbars**. Click on **Picture** so that there is a tick by it and the toolbar will be displayed.

The toolbar contains the **Wrap** buttons, the **Format Picture** and **Insert Picture** buttons and the **Reset** button (which resets the picture to its previous dimensions).

Note that the **Picture** toolbar (as with other toolbars) has slightly different buttons with web pages than with ordinary documents.

An example of text wrapping and alignment is shown below.

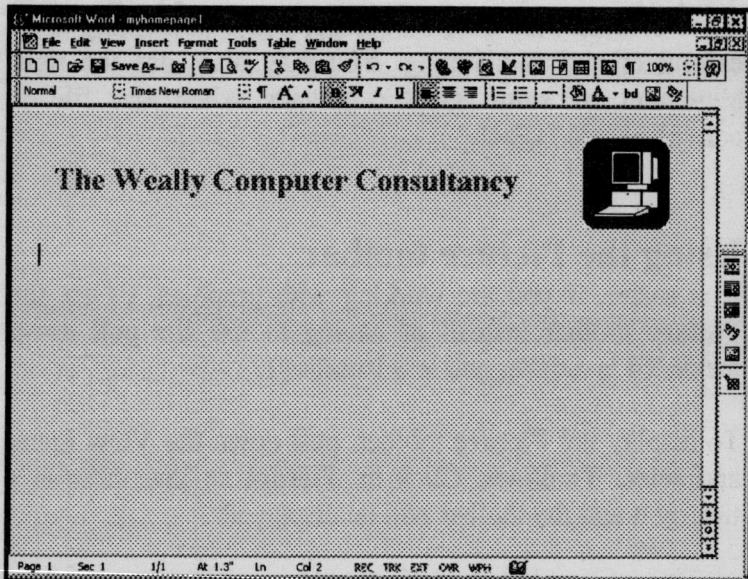

Using Picture placeholders

It is possible that the viewer will either be using a text only browser or have turned off the pictures within their browser. It is therefore sensible to enter some text that will appear in place of the picture so that the viewer has some idea of what the image showed.

This is achieved by using the **Settings** option within the **Format Picture** option.

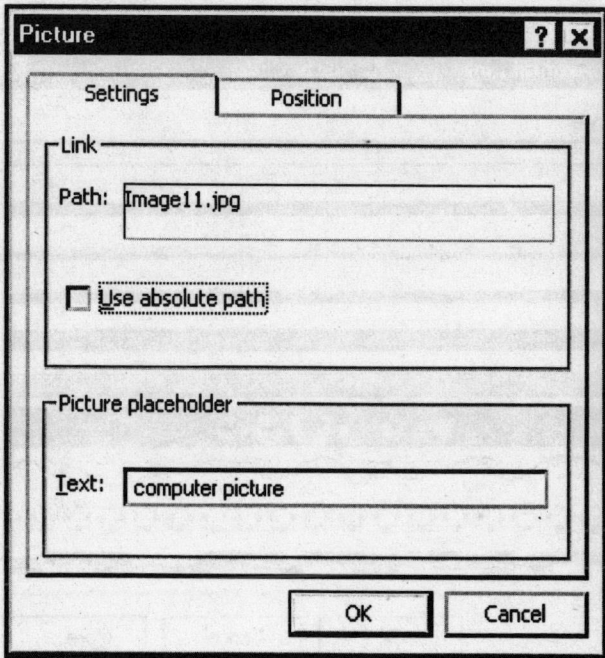

The **Link** identifies the path the browser needs to follow to find the picture, i.e. where it is stored. It may be easier to store all the pages and graphics in the same directory (folder) especially when you are starting.

Adding horizontal lines to the page

These are both decorative and allow you to break up the page. To add horizontal lines, position the cursor on the page and then click on the button. This produces the default horizontal line.

If you want one of the other available lines then pull down the **Insert** menu and select **Horizontal line**. You will see the dialog box.

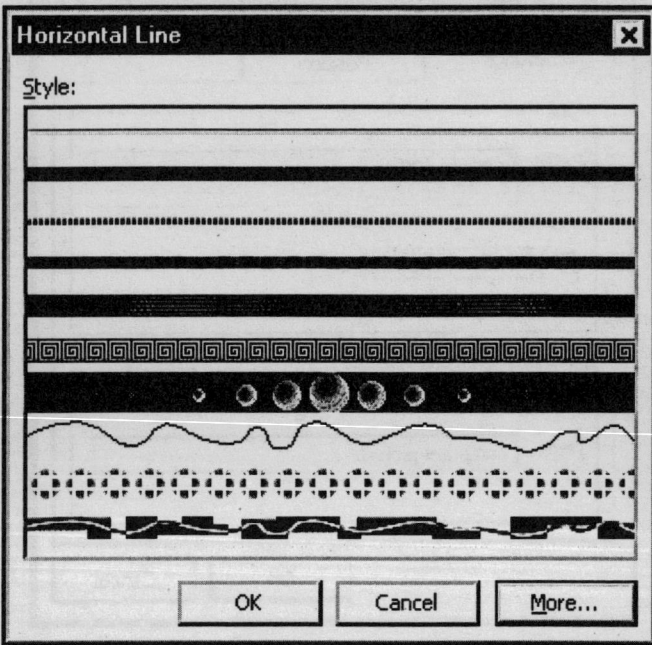

There is a **More** button and you can add any graphic you want (remember it must be in **.gif** or **.jpeg** format).

The line is a graphic and as with any graphic image, you can alter the size and position by clicking on the image to select it and then dragging the corners or sides to resize it.

You can use the **Format** (**Picture**) menu or the **Format** (**Picture**) button on the **Picture** toolbar to alter the position, wrapping and so on.

Inserting hyperlinks

The way in which you move from page to page in the World Wide Web (or indeed within a web page) is to use **Hypertext** links.

To create a hypertext link is simple. Type in the text you want to appear, highlight it and then click on the **Insert Hyperlink** button and enter the name of the HTML file you want the link to point at.

The dialog box is shown below.

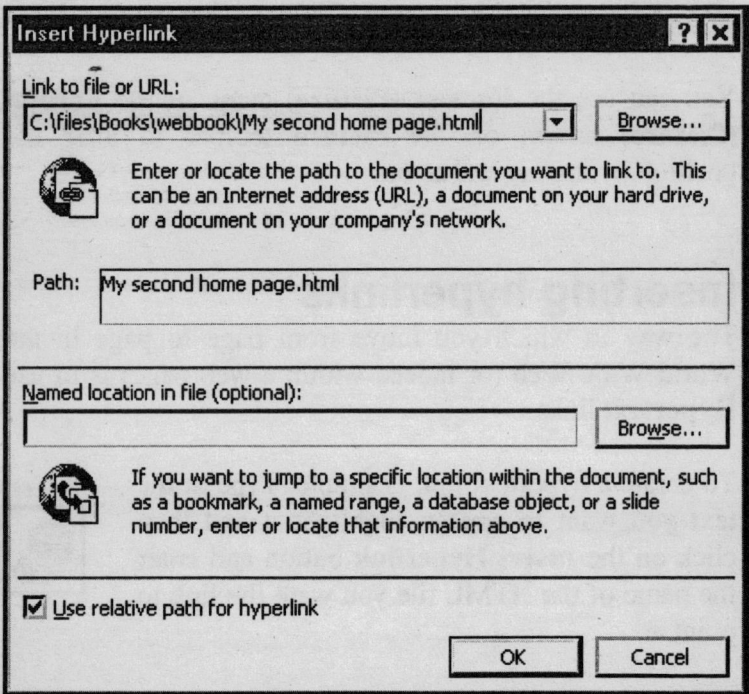

Insert Hyperlink

Link to file or URL:

C:\files\Books\webbook\My second home page.html ▼ | Browse...

Enter or locate the path to the document you want to link to. This can be an Internet address (URL), a document on your hard drive, or a document on your company's network.

Path: My second home page.html

Named location in file (optional):

Browse...

If you want to jump to a specific location within the document, such as a bookmark, a named range, a database object, or a slide number, enter or locate that information above.

☑ Use relative path for hyperlink

OK | Cancel

Notice the second part of the dialog box, you can jump to specific part of a web document (rather than jumping to the beginning of the page).

This is one of the reasons why it is important to make each page and each section within a page as self-contained and self-explanatory as possible.

Bookmarks

If you insert bookmarks into a web page, you can use them in two different ways.

❑ Insert hypertext links within the page itself, so that the link is to another part of that page (rather than to another web page).

❑ When you create a link to another page, you can make the link jump to a section within the page (rather than to the top of the page). This is described in the previous page.

To insert a bookmark, position the cursor at the point in the file where you want the bookmark, pull down the **Insert** menu and select **Bookmark**.

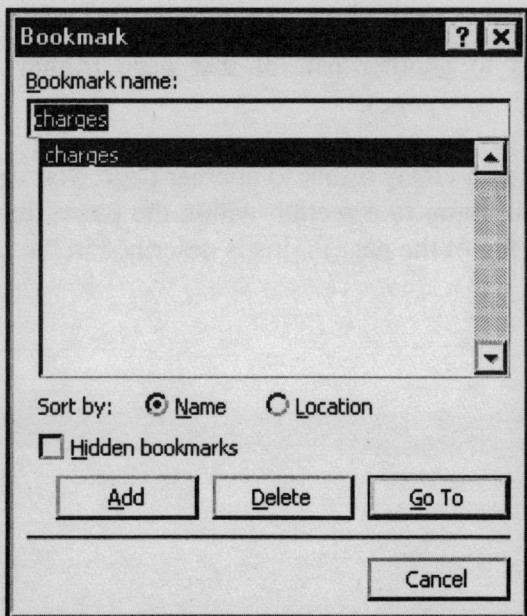

Insert the text you want to use to describe the bookmark and then click on the **Add** button.

The Pull down menus

This section deals with the commands that are **Web specific**.

File menu

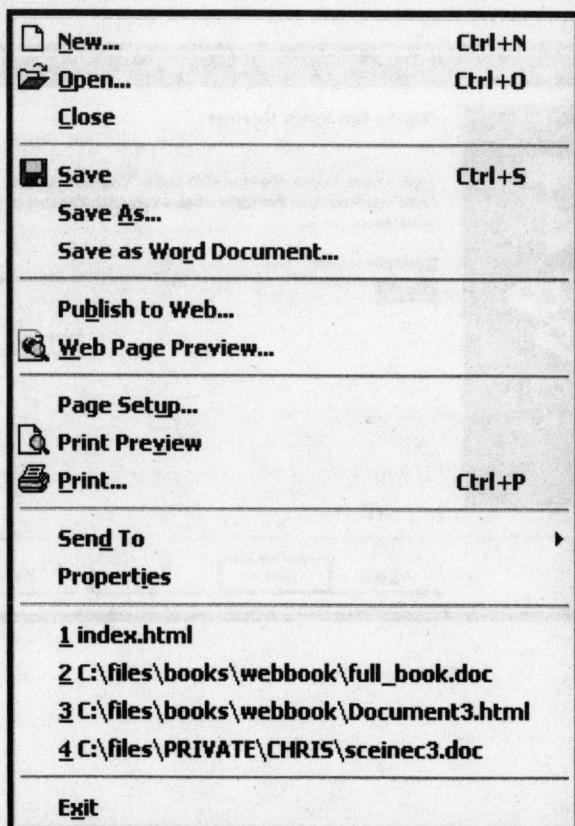

New...		Ctrl+N
Open...		Ctrl+O
Close		
Save		Ctrl+S
Save As...		
Save as Word Document...		
Publish to Web...		
Web Page Preview...		
Page Setup...		
Print Preview		
Print...		Ctrl+P
Send To		▶
Properties		
1 index.html		
2 C:\files\books\webbook\full_book.doc		
3 C:\files\books\webbook\Document3.html		
4 C:\files\PRIVATE\CHRIS\sceinec3.doc		
Exit		

Save as Word Document

You can save a hypertext document (HTML) in Word format; this is an additional file to the existing HTML file.

Publish to Web

This automates the process of uploading (sending) your pages to your information provider. The first screen you need to enter data is shown below.

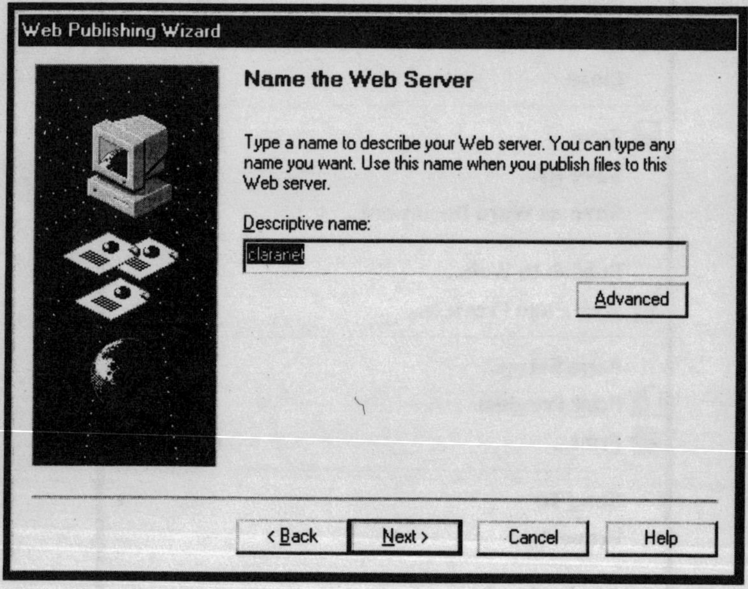

Web Publishing Wizard

Name the Web Server

Type a name to describe your Web server. You can type any name you want. Use this name when you publish files to this Web server.

Descriptive name:

claranet

Advanced

< Back | Next > | Cancel | Help

This leads to the next screen.

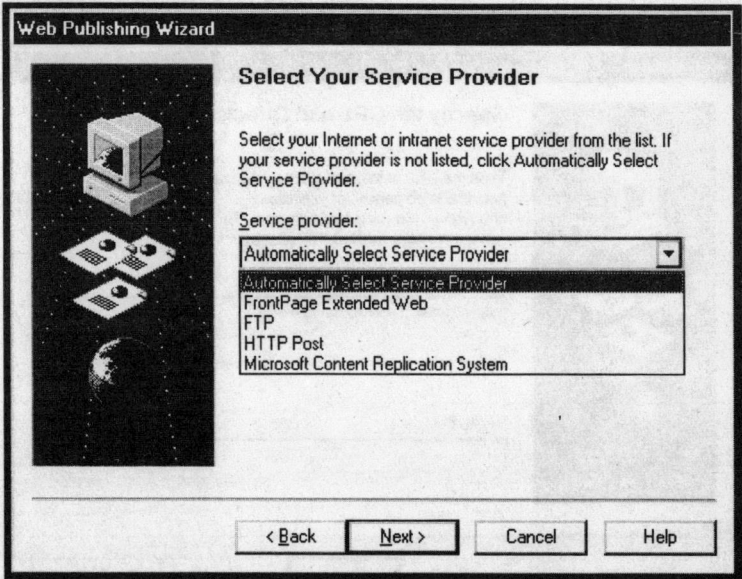

Web Publishing Wizard

Select Your Service Provider

Select your Internet or intranet service provider from the list. If
your service provider is not listed, click Automatically Select
Service Provider.

Service provider:

| Automatically Select Service Provider ▼ |

Automatically Select Service Provider
FrontPage Extended Web
FTP
HTTP Post
Microsoft Content Replication System

< Back   Next >   Cancel   Help

Here you need to choose your service provider (or leave it
to **Automatically Select**). If this does not work, you may
need to select FTP from the list. This worked for me.

Next, you need to enter the URL (which you obtain from your IP).

```
Web Publishing Wizard

                    Specify the URL and Directory

                    Type the URL or Internet address you use to access your
                    personal Web pages (for example,
                    http://www.microsoft.com/myname). Your system administrator or
                    service provider supplies this address.

                    URL or Internet address:

                    http://home.clara.net/david.weale

                    Type the local directory on your computer that will correspond
                    to the URL entered above.

                    Local directory:



                       < Back      Next >      Cancel         Help
```

This brings up the **Connect To** dialog box that connects
with your IP.

If you have problems with this, you can contact the help
line of your Information Provider.

Web Page Preview

Selecting this will automatically display the file within Microsoft Explorer. Alternatively there is a button on the toolbar.

My experience is that if you are working off-line, as you should be, it is best to load Microsoft Explorer before you use this command.

Edit menu

All the commands here are standard document commands.

View menu

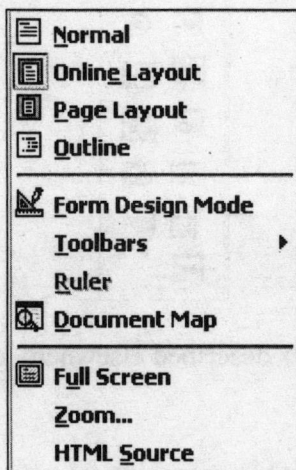

Form design mode

Selecting this displays the **Form Design** toolbar and enables you to design forms for use within your web pages.

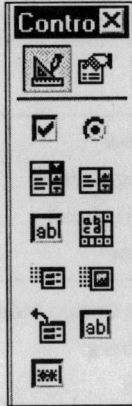

Form design itself is described elsewhere in the book.

HTML source

This lets you view the actual HTML coding for the pages you have designed. All the formatting, inserting graphics and so on are shown as HTML code.

You can edit the code if you wish to, there is a chapter later explaining this.

A page of code looks like this.

```
Microsoft Word - myhomepage1.html
File  Edit  View  Insert  Tools  Window  Help
Exit HTML Source        Save As...                          100%

<HTML>¶
<HEAD>¶
<META·HTTP-EQUIV="Content-Type"·CONTENT="text/html;·charset=windows-1252">¶
<META·NAME="Generator"·CONTENT="Microsoft·Word·97">¶
<TITLE>myhomepage1</TITLE>¶
<META·NAME="Version"·CONTENT="8.0.3410">¶
<META·NAME="Date"·CONTENT="10/11/96">¶
<META·      NAME="Template"·         CONTENT="C:\Program·      Files\Microsoft·
Office\Office\HTML.DOT">¶
</HEAD>¶
<BODY·TEXT="#000000"·LINK="#0000ff"·VLINK="#800080"·BGCOLOR="#ffff00">¶
<IMG·SRC="Image11.jpg"·ALIGN="RIGHT"·WIDTH=90·HEIGHT=90>¶
<FONT·SIZE=1·COLOR="#ff0000"><P> </FONT><FONT·SIZE=7.·COLOR="#ff0000">The·
Weally·Computer·Consultancy</P>¶
</FONT><P><IMG·SRC="line9.gif"·WIDTH=492·HEIGHT=11></P>¶
<B><FONT·SIZE=1><P> </P>¶
</FONT><FONT·SIZE=5><P>Specialising·in:</P><DIR>¶
¶
</B></FONT><P><IMG·  SRC="Bullet1.gif"·  WIDTH=12·  HEIGHT=12><B><FONT·  SIZE=4·
COLOR="#ff0000">Training</P>¶
</B></FONT><P><IMG·  SRC="Bullet1.gif"·  WIDTH=12·  HEIGHT=12><B><FONT·  SIZE=4·
COLOR="#ff0000">Web·page·development</P>¶
</FONT><FONT·SIZE=1·COLOR="#ff0000"><P> </P>¶
</FONT><FONT·SIZE=5><P><A·NAME="charges"></A>Charges·depend·upon:</P></DIR>¶
¶
<OL>¶
¶
Page 1   Sec 1        1/1      At 1"    Ln 1   Col 1      REC  TRK  EXT  OVR  WPH
```

To return to the original screens, pull down the menu again
and you will see (at the bottom) a new command **Exit
HTML source**.

49

Insert menu

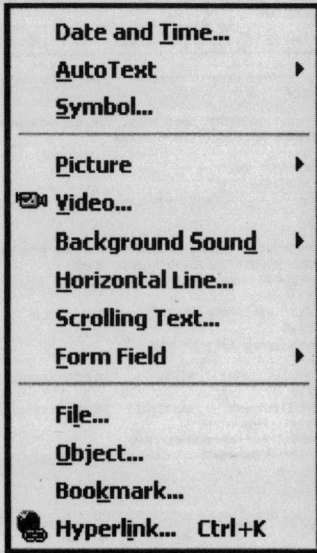

Video

It is possible to add video pictures to your web page although remember that this is processor and memory intensive as well and may take a long time to download.

```
┌─────────────────────────────────────────────────────┐
│ Video Clip                                      [×]  │
├─────────────────────────────────────────────────────┤
│ ┌─ Source ──────────────────────────────────────    │
│                                                      │
│   Video:                                             │
│   ┌──────────────────────────────┬──┐  ┌──────────┐  │
│   │ goodtime.avi                 │▼ │  │ Browse...│  │
│   └──────────────────────────────┴──┘  └──────────┘  │
│   Alternate Image:                                   │
│   ┌──────────────────────────────┬──┐  ┌──────────┐  │
│   │ logo.gif                     │▼ │  │ Browse...│  │
│   └──────────────────────────────┴──┘  └──────────┘  │
│   Alternate Text:                                    │
│   ┌──────────────────────────────────────────────┐  │
│   │ this should be a movie                       │  │
│   └──────────────────────────────────────────────┘  │
│                                                      │
│ ┌─ Playback Options ────────────────────────────     │
│                                                      │
│   Start:                                             │
│   ┌──────────────┬──┐        ☑ Display Video Controls │
│   │ Mouse-over   │▼ │                                 │
│   └──────────────┴──┘        ☑ Use Relative Paths     │
│   Loop:                                               │
│   ┌──┬──┐                    ☑ Copy to Document Folder │
│   │1 │▼ │  times                                       │
│   └──┴──┘                                              │
│                            ┌────────┐   ┌──────────┐  │
│                            │   OK   │   │  Cancel  │  │
│                            └────────┘   └──────────┘  │
└─────────────────────────────────────────────────────┘
```

Alternative Image/Text

It is always sensible to add a (static) image and alternative
text for those browsers that will not display movies; at
least the viewer has some idea of what they are missing.

Playback options

You can begin the video when the file is loaded, when the
mouse is moved over the image or both. The video can be
looped any number of times.

Display video controls
This seems sensible as the movie can be speeded up or stopped more easily, the viewer having control.

Use relative paths
This means that the video file is linked to the web page file although they are not in the same directory. There is a useful help screen on this topic.

Copy to document folder
The video (**.avi**) file is copied to the directory you are saving the web page in. This makes the links simpler and does not involve you in having the original source of the video available (for example, it may be on CD).

Note that video files can be large (and therefore slow to load); the one I used from the Microsoft Windows 95 CD was 23730 Kbytes.

An example of a page with a video clip running is shown below.

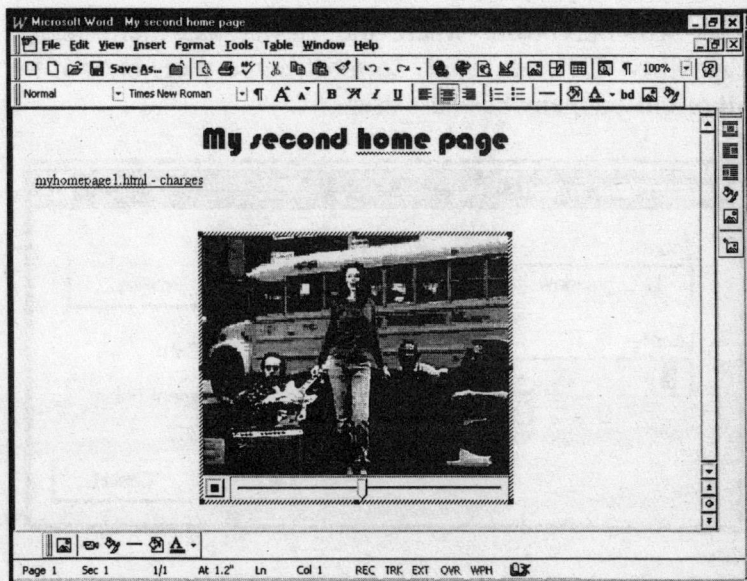

Background sound

In a similar way, you can add sound to your web pages.

This will only work where the viewer has multi-media capability. This may apply to most home users but not to all or indeed many business users.

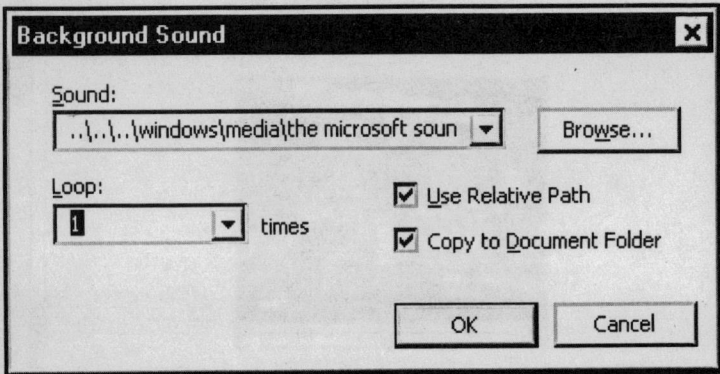

```
┌─────────────────────────────────────────────────────┐
│ Background Sound                                  [X] │
│                                                       │
│  Sound:                                               │
│  [..\..\..\windows\media\the microsoft soun [▼]]  [Browse...] │
│                                                       │
│  Loop:                      [✓] Use Relative Path     │
│  [1          [▼]]  times    [✓] Copy to Document Folder │
│                                                       │
│                        [    OK    ]  [  Cancel  ]     │
└─────────────────────────────────────────────────────┘
```

As this is a background sound, it does not show up on the page, to alter it you need to pull down the **Insert** menu again and select **Background sound**.

Horizontal line

You can insert horizontal lines within your web page, there is a variety included with the program and you can add to these if you wish. How to achieve this was dealt with earlier.

Form Field

You can design on-screen forms using the **Forms** option. Once this is selected, a further set of commands is displayed.

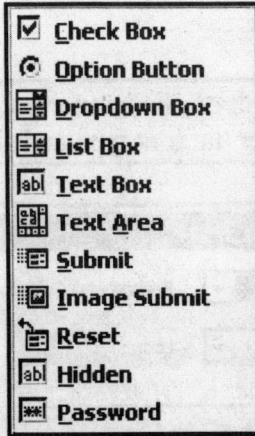

☑ **C**heck Box
⊙ **O**ption Button
▤ **D**ropdown Box
▤ **L**ist Box
abl **T**ext Box
▤ Text **A**rea
▤ **S**ubmit
▣ **I**mage Submit
▤ **R**eset
abl **H**idden
▦ **P**assword

These enable you to draw boxes on the screen and to allow an interaction with the viewer who will complete the form.

Scrolling text

This used to be called a Marquee in previous versions of the program. The dialog box is simple to use.

Enter your text and the various options, a sample is shown within the dialog box.

To alter the font, click on the banner once it is in the page and you can then alter the font type and size as you wish.

Scrolling Text

Behavior: Scroll

Background Color: Yellow

Direction: Left

Loop: Infinite

Speed

Slow — Fast

Type the Scrolling Text Here:

welcome to my world

Preview

welcome to m

OK   Cancel

Format menu

```
A  Font...
:=  Bullets and Numbering...
    Text Colors...
    ─────────────────────
    Change Case...
    ─────────────────────
    Style...
    Background...              ▶
    Picture...
```

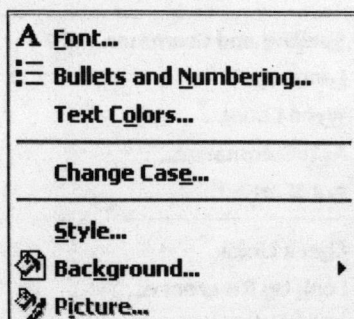

All of these have been dealt with elsewhere or are standard
document commands.

Tools menu

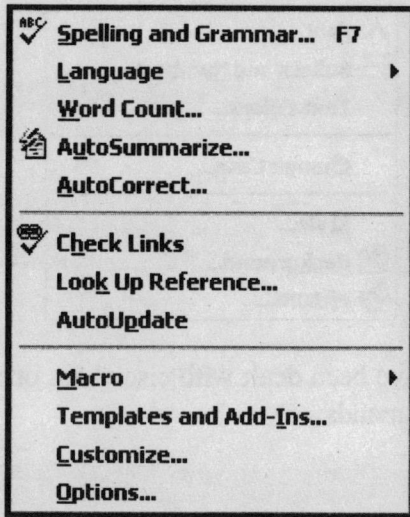

Check links

This checks that the hyperlinks you have used within your web page actually exist. If they are incorrect, you will get the following message. You can then alter the link as necessary.

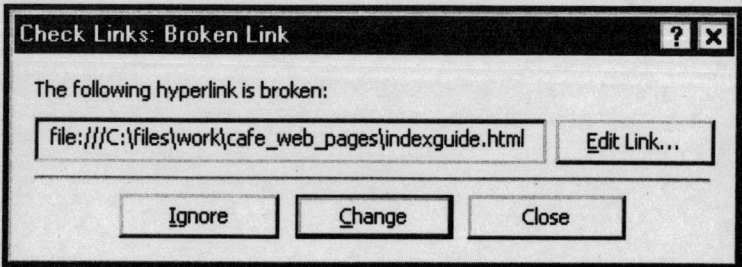

AutoUpdate

A useful feature, you can download the latest version of the Microsoft web authoring tools form the Internet, this command connects with the Microsoft web site.

Table menu

✎	Draw Ta**b**le
⊒+⊏	**I**nsert Rows
	Delete Cells...
▦	**M**erge Cells
▦	S**p**lit Cells...
	Tabl**e** Properties...
	Ce**ll** Properties...
	B**o**rders...
	Select **R**ow
	Select **C**olumn
	Select T**a**ble
⊒‡	Distribute Rows Eve**n**ly
⊞	Distribute Columns Evenl**y**
	Con**v**ert Text to Table...
⚄↓	**S**ort...
	Split **T**able
▦	Hide **G**ridlines

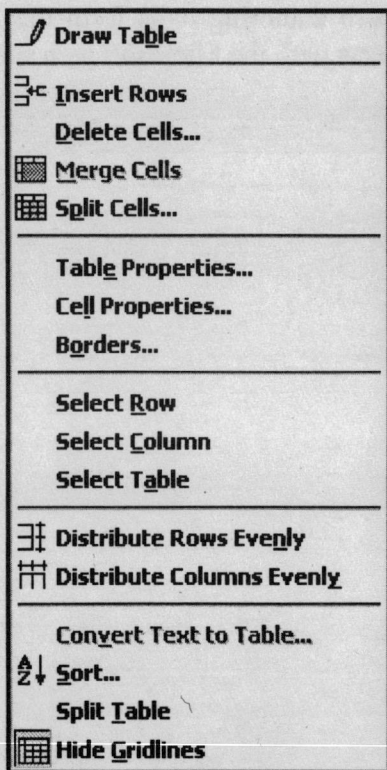

A table is one of the best ways of making sure text lines up and looks good on the page. Even if you have not used tables much before I strongly suggest you use them in your web pages.

Table properties

You can alter the text wrapping around the table and the distance of the table from the text as well as alter the space between the columns.

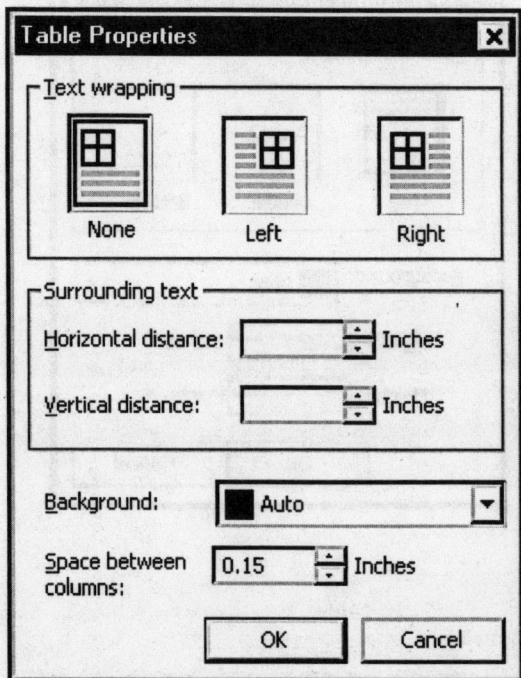

Cell properties

Similarly, you can alter the alignment, background colour, width and height of the cells within a table.

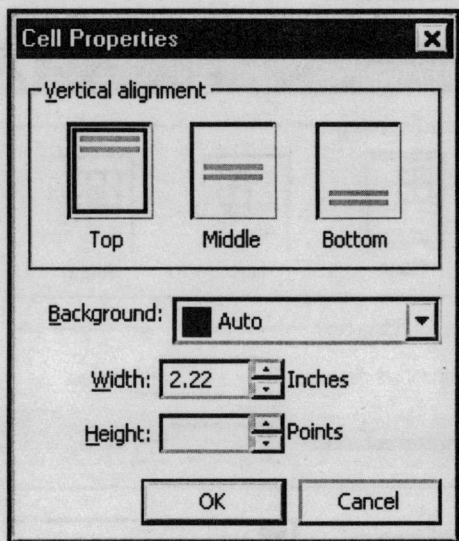

Borders

You can alter the way the borders in your table (or cell) look by using this command.

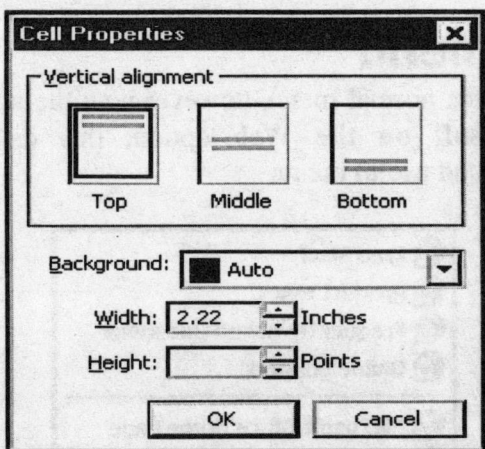

Window menu

This is the same as the standard menu.

Help menu

Similar to the normal menu, however note the addition of the **Microsoft on the Web** option, this displays an interesting and useful menu.

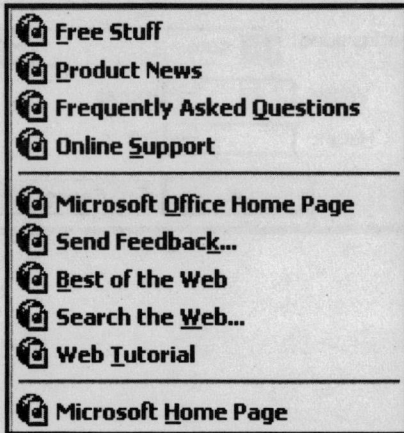

🌐 *F*ree Stuff
🌐 *P*roduct News
🌐 *F*requently Asked *Q*uestions
🌐 Online *S*upport
🌐 Microsoft *O*ffice Home Page
🌐 Send Feedbac*k*...
🌐 *B*est of the Web
🌐 Search the *W*eb...
🌐 Web *T*utorial
🌐 Microsoft *H*ome Page

Creating Forms

Forms can be used in web pages to collect data.

You can use the **Web Page Wizard** (selecting one of the form options) to help you create the form and then modify it if you wish.

You can also create your own forms by clicking on the various buttons and adding them to a web page, you must include a **Submit** button if you want the results.

Creating your own forms

If you want to create your own forms, I suggest you pull down the **View** menu and from the toolbars, select the **Forms** toolbar.

Note that this contains fewer buttons and facilities than the Forms toolbar you would see if you were working with a normal (not Web) page.

If you pull down the **View** and select **Form Design Mode**, this will display the **Forms Control** toolbar, which you can use to add features to your form.

Both of these are used to create the forms you want to design.

Using the wizard to create forms

Start a new file by pulling down the **File** menu and selecting **New**. Then click the **Web Page** tab and select **Web Page Wizard**.

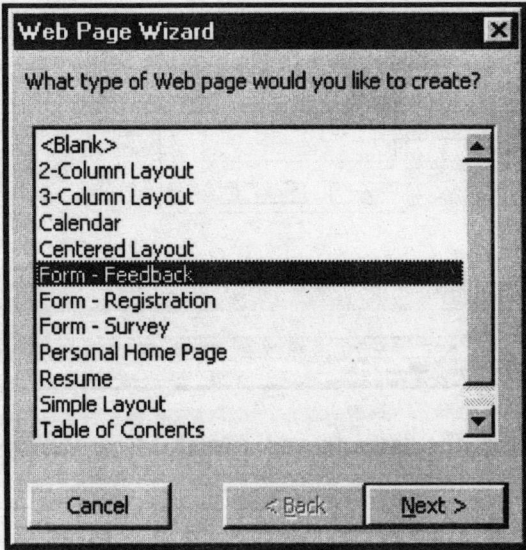

You will see there is a choice of forms. Select one and move to the next screen.

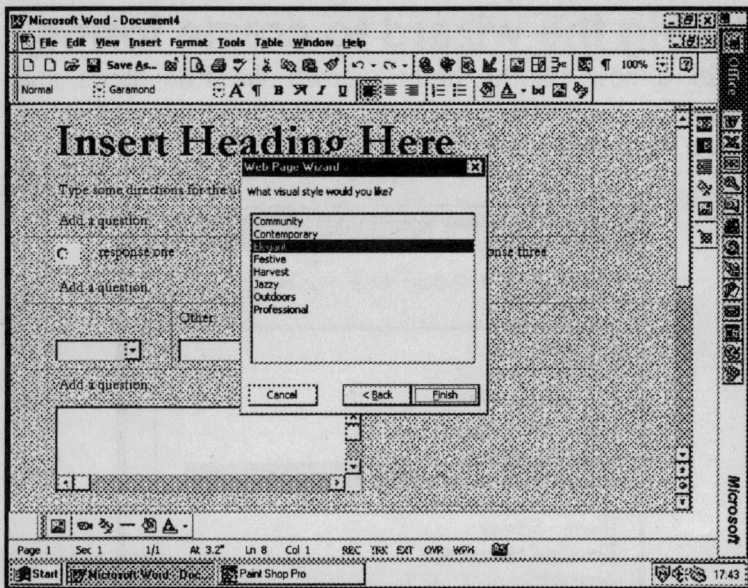

Insert Heading Here

Type some directions for the u...

Add a question.

C response one ...onse three

Add a question.

Other:

Add a question.

Web Page Wizard

What visual style would you like?

Community
Contemporary
Elegant
Festive
Harvest
Jazzy
Outdoors
Professional

Cancel   < Back   Finish

Choose from the layouts and **Finish**. You will see your form on the screen.

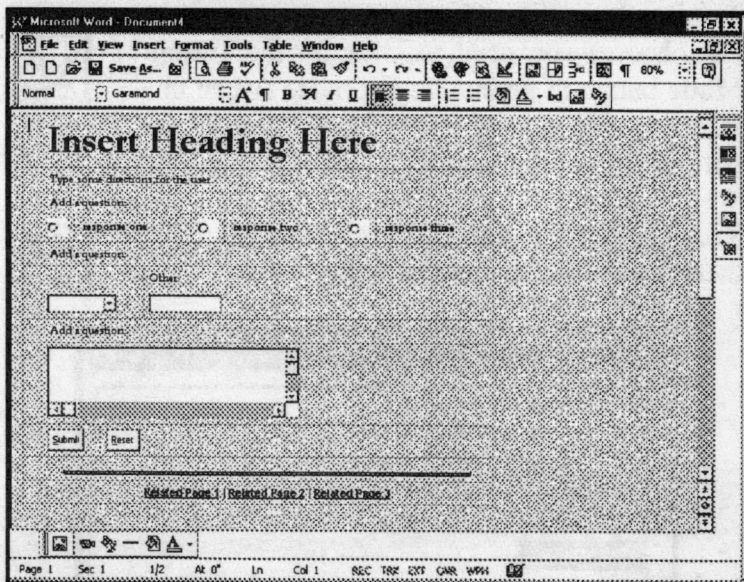

You can now modify it as you wish.

Modifying a form

You can alter any of the elements of a form.

Text

Simply highlight the text you want to replace and over-type.

Drop down boxes

These are boxes with an arrow to the right. By clicking on the arrow, you pull down a list of alternative answers, from which one is chosen.

To alter the options (from which the respondent can choose) you need to click on the **Design Mode** button to go into design mode (when this is active you should see a small icon to the bottom right of the screen).

Then click on the drop down box to select it and then click on the **Properties** button.

Properties	✕
HTMLSelect1 HTMLSelect	▼

Alphabetic	Categorized

(Name)	HTMLSelect1
DisplayValues	yes;no;maybe
HTMLName	
MultiSelect	False
Selected	
Size	1
Values	Option 1;no;maybe

Enter the data you want displayed for each of the options in the **DisplayValues** box, separating each by a semi-colon (but no spaces).

On-line forms

You can include forms in your web page so the reader can submit responses to you. This requires certain facilities to be available on the web server and you need to ensure that the results can be sent to you.

For example you need to know what interface your server operates (in order to receive data from Web users). It may be either the Internet Database Connector (Windows NT) or the Common Gateway Interface (CGI).

Excel

Some Ideas

Some of the things you can do with Excel and the Internet are:

❑ Publish your workbooks as web pages.

❑ Include hyperlinks in your own workbooks (link to other pages on the Internet or company Intranet).

❑ You can open (other people's) workbooks that are available on the Internet and on your company Intranet.

Workbooks as web pages

Once you have created a workbook, you can save it as an HTML file by clicking on the **File** menu and selecting **Save as HTML**.

This will begin the **Wizard** that will guide you through the process.

The first stage is to decide upon the cell range you want to publish on the web.

Look at the range identified in the Wizard, you can alter this by clicking on the **Add** button and highlighting the cell ranges you want to include.

To remove ranges, simply identify the range by selecting it within the Wizard and clicking on the **Remove** button.

You can also move the sequence in which the ranges are displayed using the **Move** button.

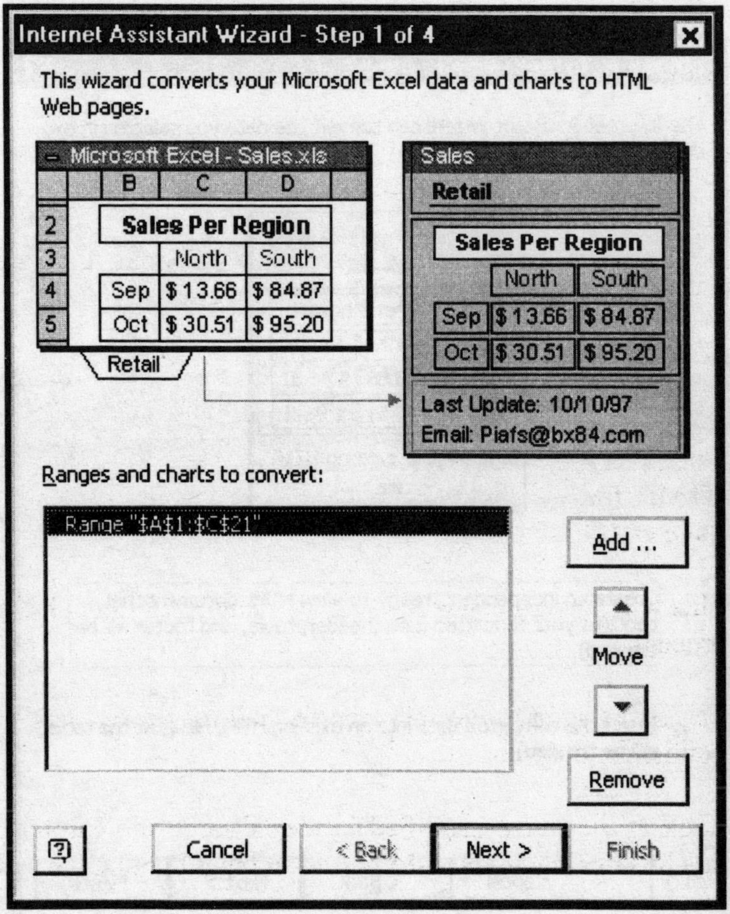

Internet Assistant Wizard - Step 1 of 4
This wizard converts your Microsoft Excel data and charts to HTML Web pages.
Microsoft Excel - Sales.xls
B
C
D
2
3
4
5
Sales Per Region
North
South
Sep
$ 13.66
$ 84.87
Oct
$ 30.51
$ 95.20
Retail
Sales
Retail
Sales Per Region
North
South
Sep
$ 13.66
$ 84.87
Oct
$ 30.51
$ 95.20
Last Update: 10/10/97
Email: Piafs@bx84.com
Ranges and charts to convert:
Range "$A$1:$C$21"
Add ...
Move
Remove
Cancel
< Back
Next >
Finish

The next step is to decide whether to create a new web page or to incorporate the worksheet data into an existing web page.

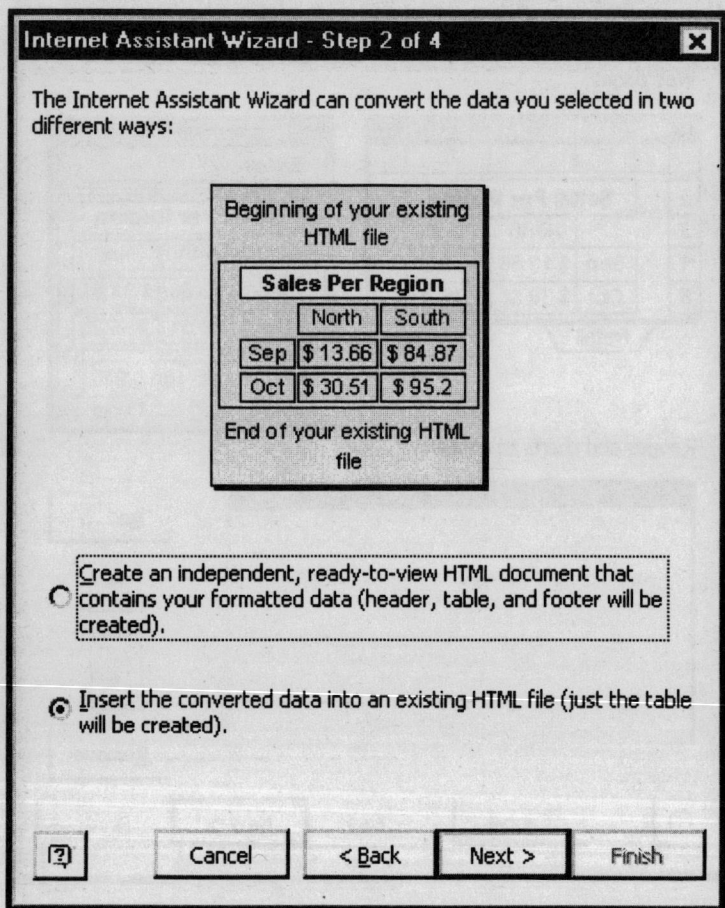

Depending upon your choice here, the next screen will be different. The choices are dealt with below (**Independent HTML document** and **Inserting data or charts**).

Independent HTML document

If you decide to create a separate web page then you will see an additional screen (shown below).

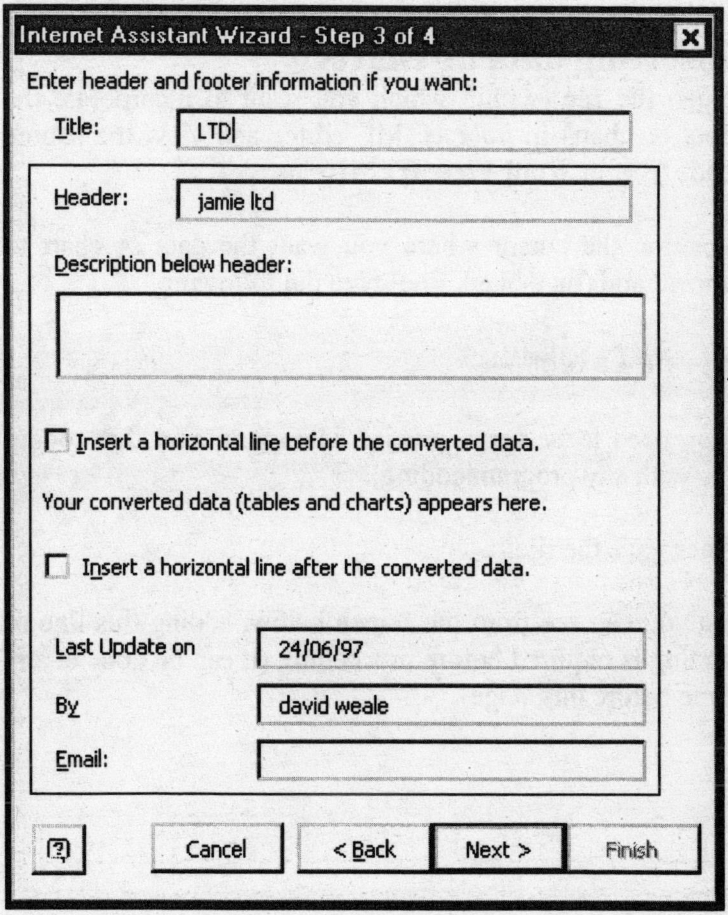

At this stage, you can add or alter the information and make various changes to the layout.

Note that some features of Excel may not convert successfully to HTML format (for more information call up the help screens).

Inserting data or charts

Open the file (within which you want to incorporate the data or chart) in your HTML editor and view the source code (e.g. in Word **View HTML Source**).

Position the cursor where you want the data or chart to appear and (on a blank line) type the following

<!--##Table##-->

You need to be **very** precise when you enter this coding (as with any program coding).

Then save the file.

As you can see from the screen below, adding this line of coding is required before proceeding (it can be done at any time before this stage).

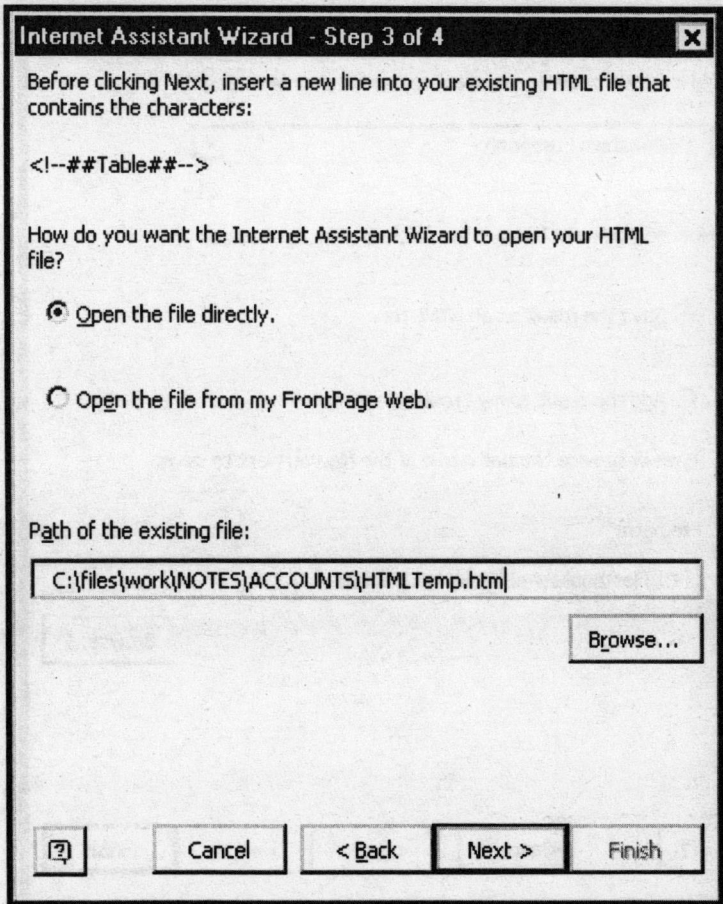

Before clicking Next, insert a new line into your existing HTML file that contains the characters:

<!--##Table##-->

How do you want the Internet Assistant Wizard to open your HTML file?

◉ Open the file directly.

○ Open the file from my FrontPage Web.

Path of the existing file:

C:\files\work\NOTES\ACCOUNTS\HTMLTemp.htm

Browse...

| ? | Cancel | < Back | Next > | Finish |

Next step

Whichever choice you made you will then see the following screen (step 4).

Be careful when choosing the path to ensure you save the file in the directory (folder) that you want to.

Internet Assistant Wizard - Step 4 of 4 ✕

Which code page do you want to use for your Web page?

| US/Western European ▼ |

How do you want to save the finished HTML Web page?

◉ Save the result as an HTML file.

○ Add the result to my FrontPage Web.

Type or browse the pathname of the file you want to save.

File path:

| C:\files\books\webbook\MyHTML.htm |

Browse...

| ? | Cancel | < Back | Next > | Finish |

The file is then saved as an HTML file (hypertext mark-up language) and can be viewed using a web browser (e.g. Microsoft Explorer).

You may need to watch the size of the tables (figures) and charts in the finished pages as they can be too large to view easily.

You can alter the size either by opening the saved file in Word and using the **Format**, **Picture** commands or by altering the HTML code (see chapter on HTML Coding).

Adding hyperlinks to a worksheet

To include a hyperlink within your worksheet (to another web page or site), pull down the **Insert** menu and select **Hyperlink**. You will see the following dialog.

Insert Hyperlink	? X

Link to file or URL:

[▼] [Browse...]

Enter or locate the path to the document you want to link to. This can be an Internet address (URL), a document on your hard drive, or a document on your company's network.

Path: <Link to containing document>

Named location in file (optional):

[   ] [Browse...]

If you want to jump to a specific location within the document, such as a bookmark, a named range, a database object, or a slide number, enter or locate that information above.

☑ Use relative path for hyperlink

[OK]   [Cancel]

The link will be inserted into the worksheet wherever the cursor is positioned at the time. You can only insert hyperlinks in worksheets, not in charts.

Opening other HTML files

You can open other workbooks held on your company Intranet or from the Internet and view them as an Excel worksheet.

Any HTML file can be opened within Excel (though the formatting may look different, not to say odd).

To do so, open the file as you normally would (make sure that you have altered the **Files of type** to HTML files and alter it back when you want to open Excel files).

Getting External Data

You can add data from other sources to your Excel web pages by pulling down the **Data** menu and selecting **Get External Data**.

You are given a choice.

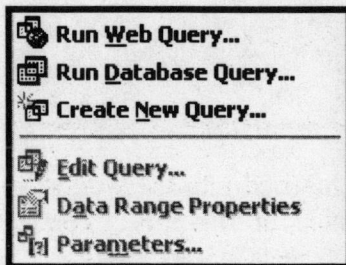

📇 Run **W**eb Query...
📇 Run **D**atabase Query...
📇 Create **N**ew Query...
📇 **E**dit Query...
📇 D**a**ta Range Properties
📇 Para**m**eters...

There are several sites already set up, you can add to these by selecting **Creating New Query**. The screen for **Run Web Query** is shown for reference.

Look in: Queries

Detailed Stock Quote by PC Quote, Inc.iqy
Dow Jones Stocks by PC Quote, Inc.iqy
Get More Web Queries.iqy
Multiple Stock Quotes by PC Quote, Inc.iqy

Get Data

Cancel

File name:

Files of type: Web Queries (*.iqy)

4 file(s) found.

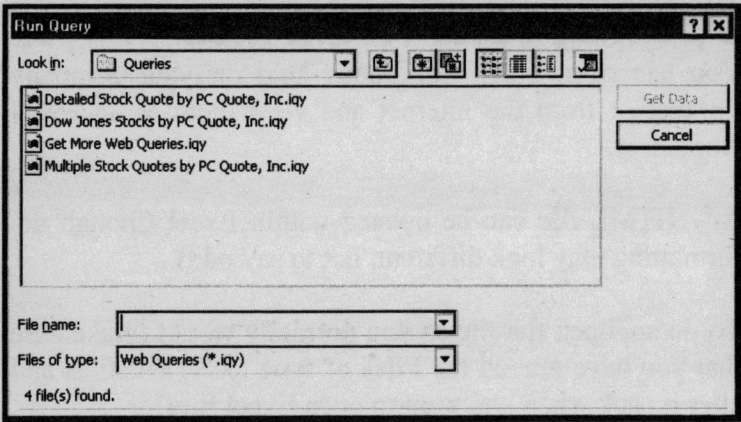

Use a form to obtain data

You can create a form to obtain data from anyone viewing your web pages. This is achieved by using the **Tools** toolbar (dealt with in the sections dealing with Word).

PowerPoint

Existing presentations

You can save any existing presentation in HTML and convert your existing presentation into a series of web pages.

The **Wizard** is described below (**Saving a PowerPoint file as HTML**).

Online templates

Use these to create web presentations from scratch.

When you start the program, select **Template** from the dialog box.

However, if you are already using PowerPoint and want to use the templates to create web pages, pull down the **File** menu and select **New**.

You will see that there is a choice. Click on the **Presentations** tab and the various (both normal and on-line) presentation templates will be shown.

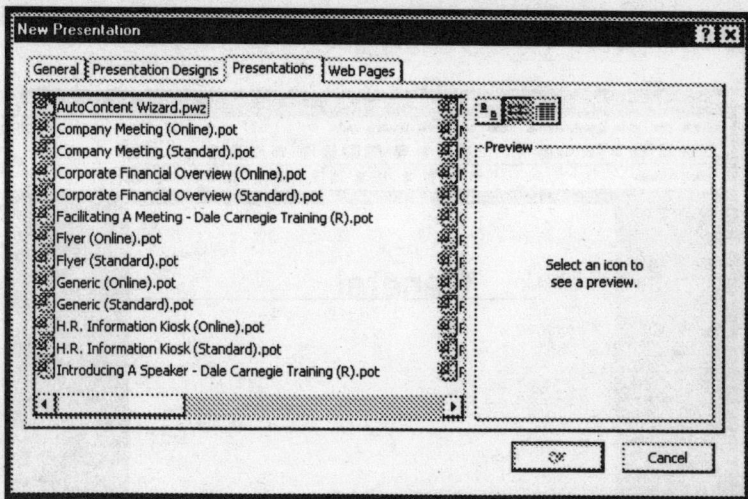

Note the three buttons on the right, these allow you to look at the list in different ways (as icons, as a list and as a list in more detail).

You choose (an on-line template) from the list (remember that you can preview each by clicking on the title and you can see how it looks in the preview box to the right).

It is a good idea to look closely at the list, as there are a variety of different business and personal on-line templates. Remember that a template is only a starting point and you can alter the finished result if you wish to.

Then create your presentation normally and save it as an HTML file by pulling down the **File** menu and selecting **Save as HTML**.

An example of an on-line template is shown below.

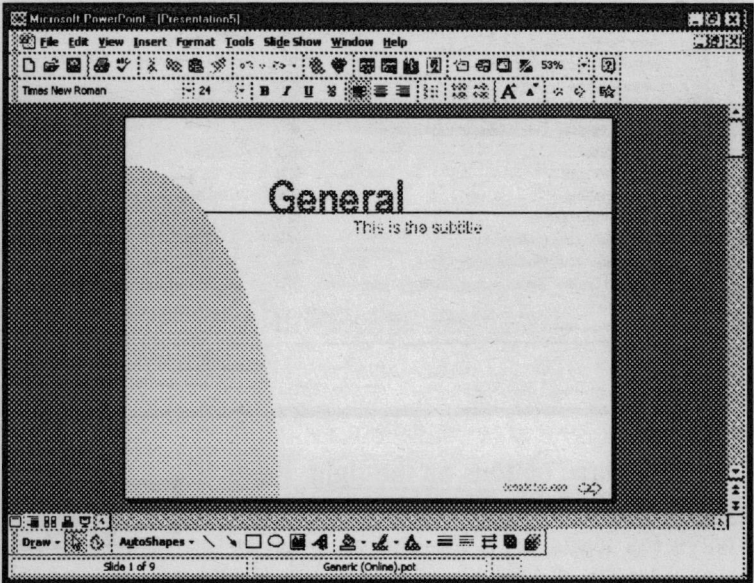

Saving a PowerPoint file as HTML

You can save your file using the **File** menu, followed by **Save as HTML**. There is a **Wizard** to assist you.

I have illustrated most of the **Wizard** screens and added explanations as they illustrate some fundamental points about creating web pages in PowerPoint.

The initial screen is shown below.

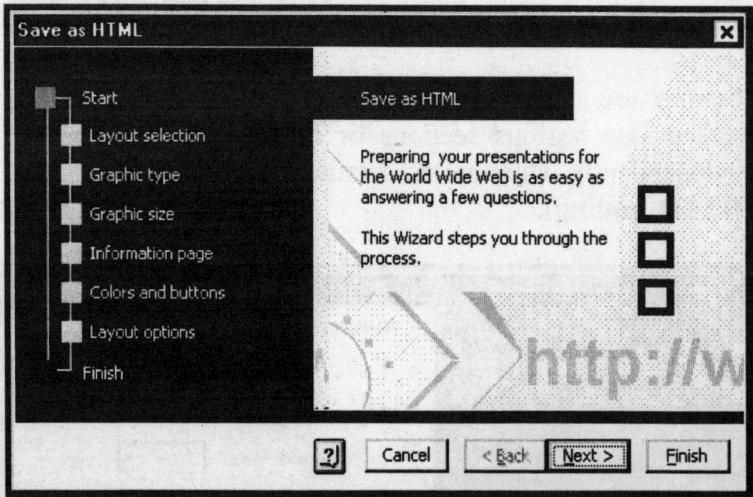

This is followed by several screens asking you to make various choices. Some are illustrated and explained below.

The **page style** can be altered to **Browser frames**. This is a more sophisticated display and may not display properly in older versions of the browsers.

Frames are used where the designer wants to split the screen into various sections or frames that can operate independently (for more details, read the chapter on **HTML coding**).

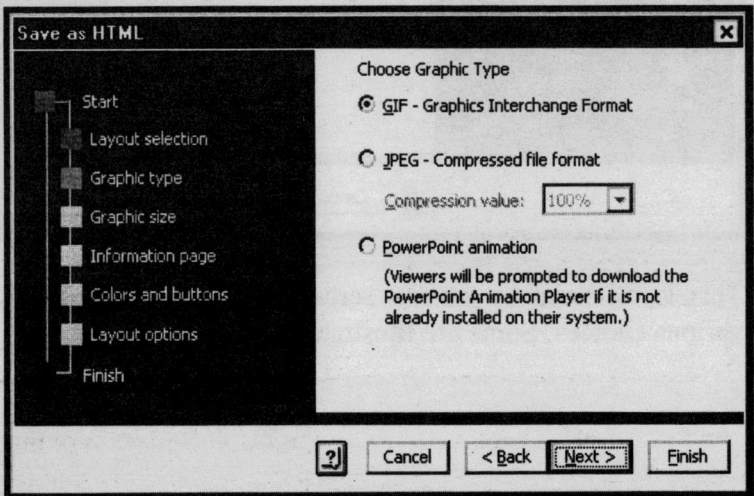

The graphics format you choose defines the quality of the image and its file size (GIF files tend to be better quality but may be larger in size, the quality and size of JPEG files depends upon the compression ratio - the higher the quality, the larger the size of file).

With graphics, there is always a trade off between file size, therefore the speed with which they can be viewed, and the quality of the image.

Note the third option, you can create web pages which retain and display the builds as part of the web page (the viewer may need to download a free Microsoft program to view the builds and they will automatically be prompted to do so).

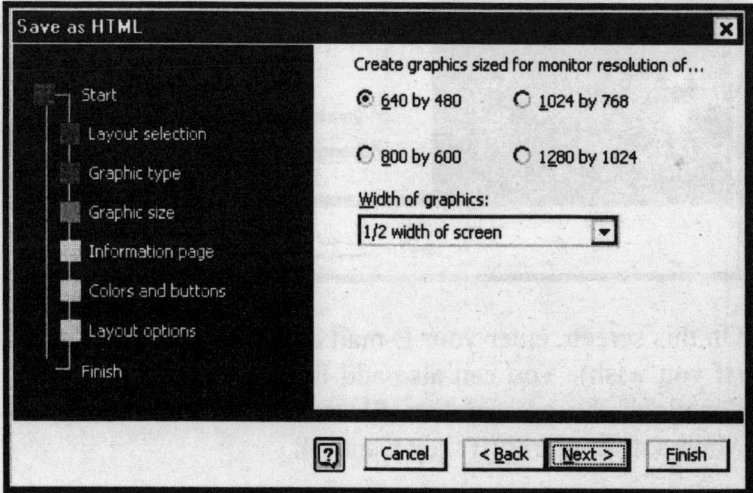

Be **very** careful here, if you alter the resolution be sure that the people viewing your web pages are operating at that (or a higher) resolution. Otherwise, they may only be able to see part of the image at any time.

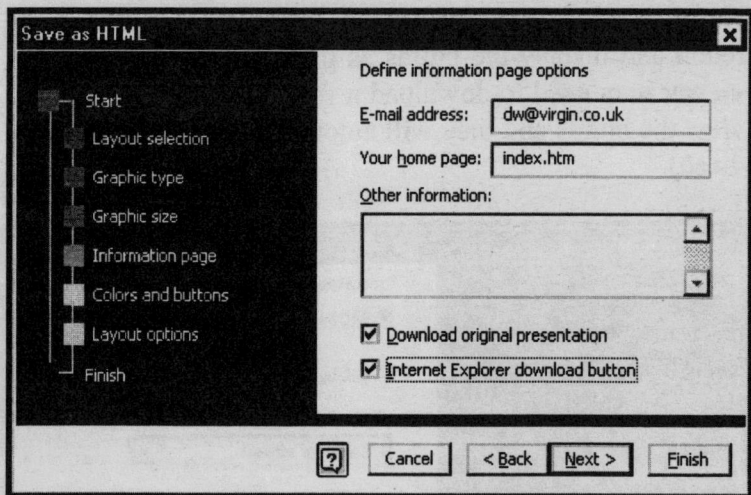

Save as HTML

Define information page options

E-mail address: `dw@virgin.co.uk`

Your home page: `index.htm`

Other information:

☑ Download original presentation
☑ Internet Explorer download button

- Start
- Layout selection
- Graphic type
- Graphic size
- Information page
- Colors and buttons
- Layout options
- Finish

Cancel   < Back   Next >   Finish

On this screen, enter your E-mail address and a home page (if you wish). You can also add links to allow the user to download the presentation file and the latest version of Microsoft Explorer (if they want to).

The next page lets you alter the colours (the default is to use the browser colours as set by the viewer).

The template automatically adds buttons, here you can choose the style.

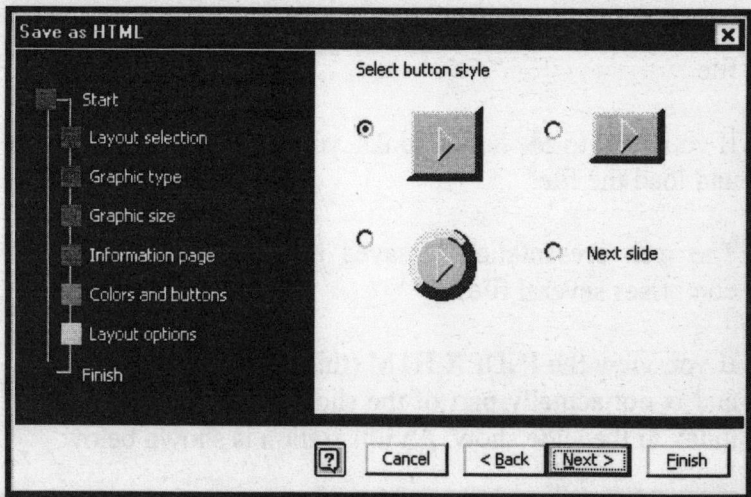

Save as HTML

Select button style

- Start
- Layout selection
- Graphic type
- Graphic size
- Information page
- Colors and buttons
- Layout options
- Finish

Next slide

[?] Cancel < Back Next > Finish

This screen lets you decide where to place the buttons that you chose in the previous screen.

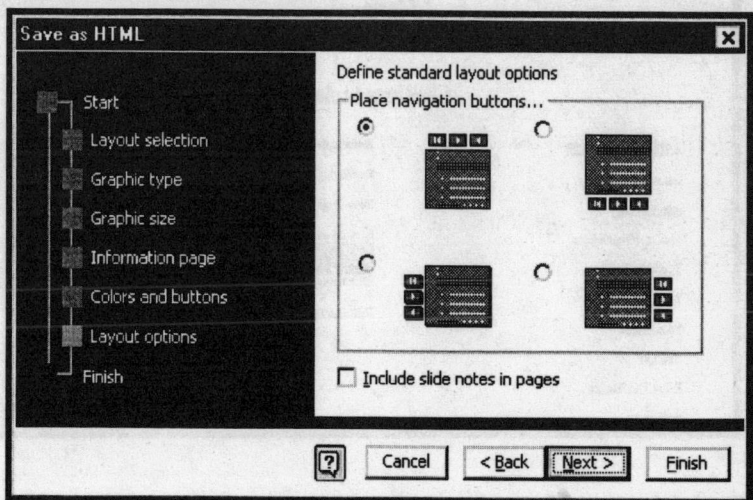

Save as HTML

Define standard layout options

Place navigation buttons...

- Start
- Layout selection
- Graphic type
- Graphic size
- Information page
- Colors and buttons
- Layout options
- Finish

☐ Include slide notes in pages

[?] Cancel < Back Next > Finish

The final screen requires you to choose where to save the file.

If you want to see how it looks, you can open your browser and load the file.

The web presentation is saved in its own directory and comprises several files.

If you view the INDEX.HTM (this is created automatically and is not actually part of the slide show), you will see an index to the slide show. An illustration is shown below.

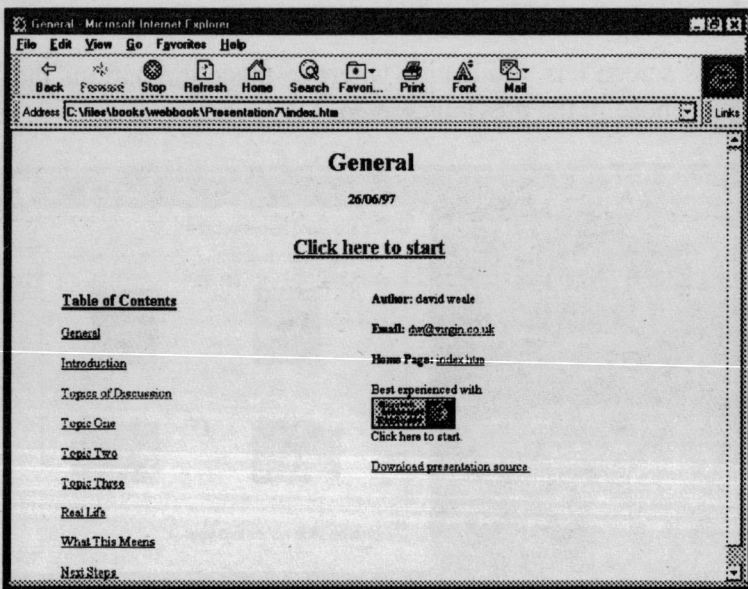

If you click on the **Click here to start** hyperlink then the slide show itself will begin.

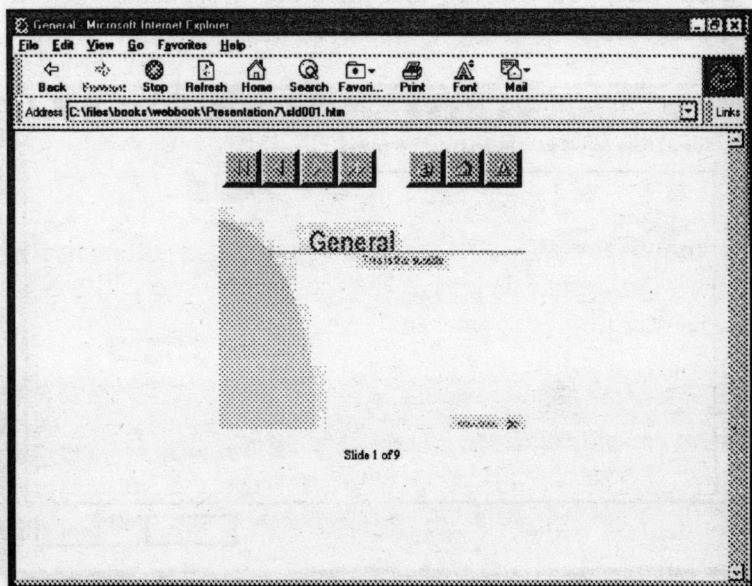

Note the **text** link, you can look at a text version of the slide if you want to speed things up or the browser being used does not support images.

Banners

Another option within **File New** is **Web Pages**. If you select this, you will see that there are two banner files to choose from.

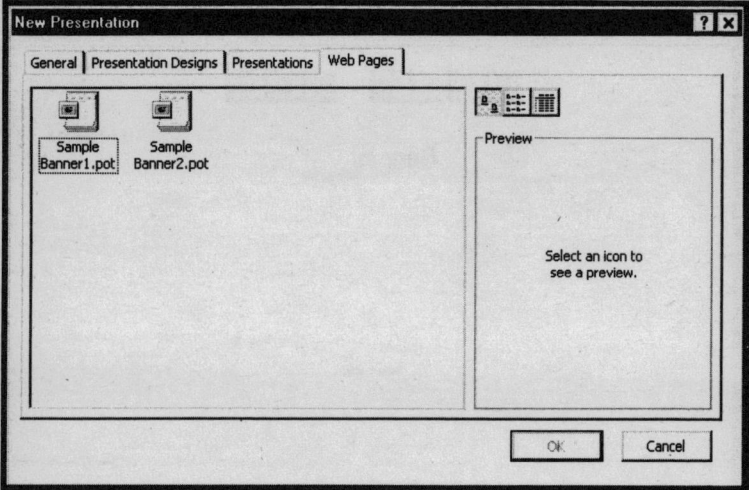

You can alter these banners as you wish and then save as HTML files to display on a browser. Each file consists of three slides, each with a different banner.

An example is shown below.

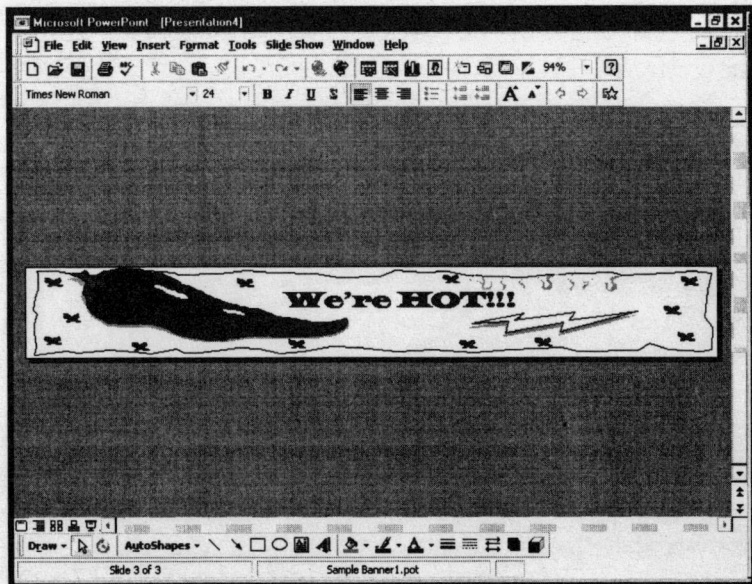

Access

The Access Web Wizard

You can save any Access Table, Form, Report, Query or Datasheets as HTML. You begin this process by pulling down the file menu and selecting **Save As HTML**.

This starts the Web Wizard.

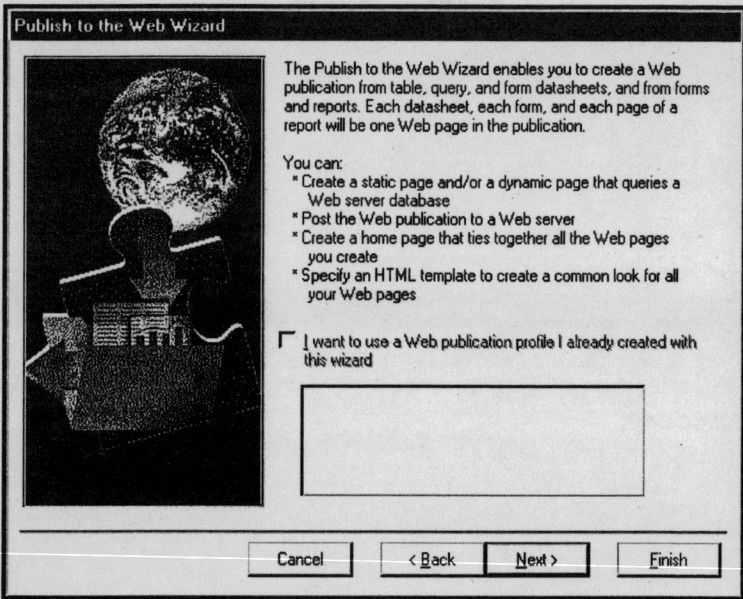

You can save any combination of tables, or queries.

To do this select the item you are interested in and click on the **Select** button on the right of the dialog box. Doing this will leave a tick to the left of the item.

You can move between Tables, Queries, and Forms and so on by clicking the tabs along the top.

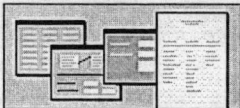

Publish to the Web Wizard

You can publish any combination of tables, queries, forms, and reports.

What do you want to publish?

Tables | Queries | Forms | Reports | All Objects

- ☑ cds to look for
- ☐ saleitems
- ☐ top100albums
- ☐ top50
- ☑ cds to look for Query
- ☑ cds to look for Query
- ☑ cds to look for Query

Deselect

Select All

Deselect All

Cancel | < Back | Next > | Finish

After selecting the item(s) you want to use, the next screen is shown.

An HTML template can provide some formatting for your Web pages, such as a background pattern, navigation buttons, logos, and text.

What HTML document (.htm or .html file), if any, do you want to use as a default template?

| | Browse... |

☐ I want to select different templates for some of the selected objects.

| Cancel | < Back | Next > | Finish |

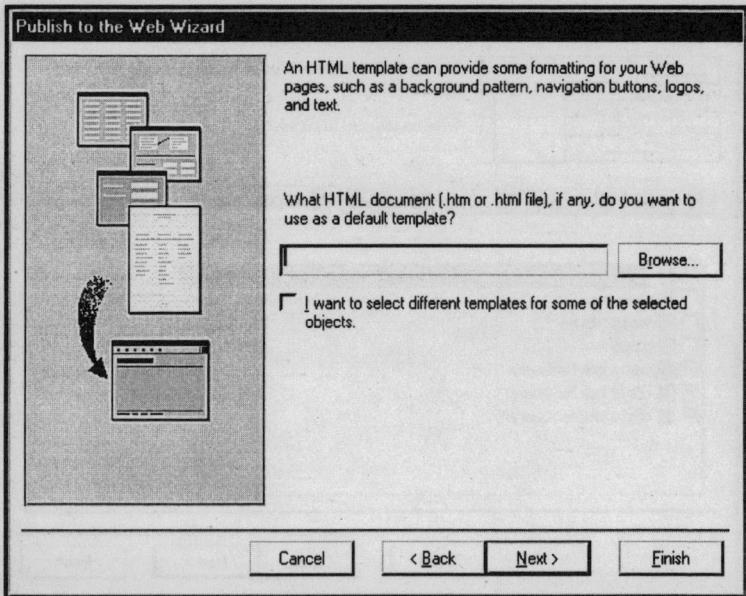

You need to choose an HTML template (if you **Browse**, you should see the display below, simply select a template).

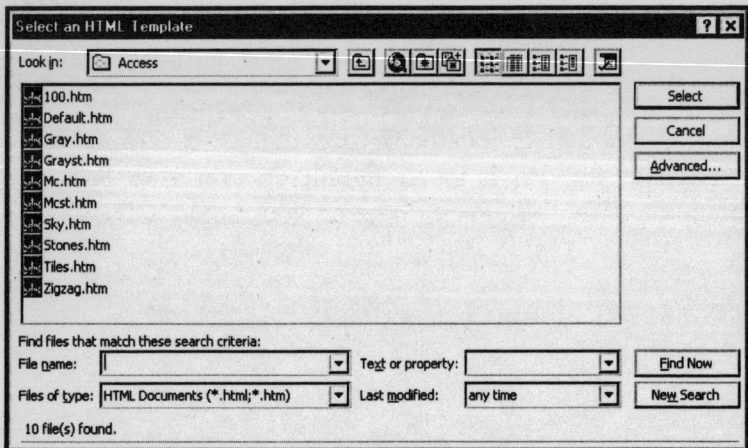

Select an HTML Template   ? ✕

Look in: ☐ Access

100.htm
Default.htm
Gray.htm
Grayst.htm
Mc.htm
Mcst.htm
Sky.htm
Stones.htm
Tiles.htm
Zigzag.htm

| Select |
| Cancel |
| Advanced... |

Find files that match these search criteria:

File name: | | Text or property: | | Find Now |

Files of type: HTML Documents (*.html;*.htm) | Last modified: any time | New Search |

10 file(s) found.

Moving onto the next screen.

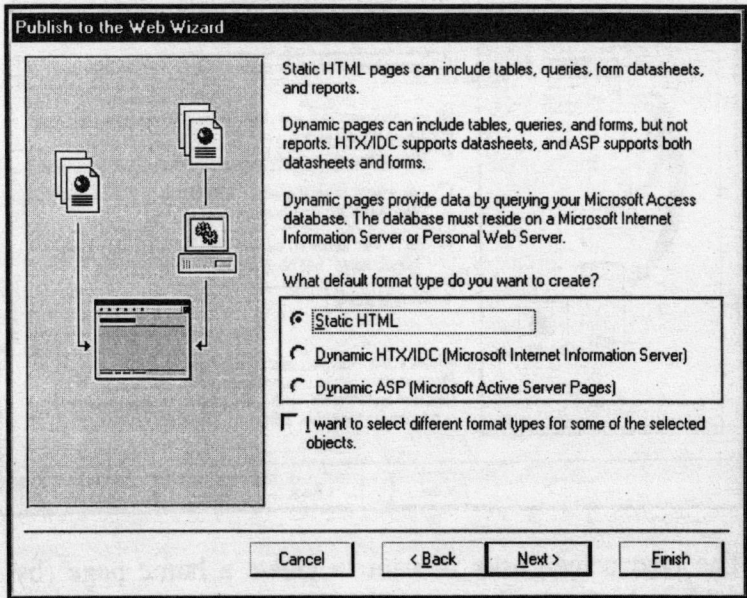

```
Publish to the Web Wizard

        Static HTML pages can include tables, queries, form datasheets,
        and reports.

        Dynamic pages can include tables, queries, and forms, but not
        reports. HTX/IDC supports datasheets, and ASP supports both
        datasheets and forms.

        Dynamic pages provide data by querying your Microsoft Access
        database. The database must reside on a Microsoft Internet
        Information Server or Personal Web Server.

        What default format type do you want to create?

        (•) Static HTML
        ( ) Dynamic HTX/IDC (Microsoft Internet Information Server)
        ( ) Dynamic ASP (Microsoft Active Server Pages)

        [ ] I want to select different format types for some of the selected
            objects.


        Cancel        < Back      Next >          Finish
```

For the purposes of this book, we will stay with static
pages, however if you have your own server then it is
worth looking at dynamic.

You then choose where to save the page and whether you
want to publish it locally or use the **Web Publishing
Wizard** to publish it to an Internet Server (the Wizard
should be in the ValuPack folder on your Office CD).

103

Where do you want to publish to?

I want to put my Web publication in this folder:

C:\files\books\webbook\images   Browse...

Do you also want to publish to an Internet Server using the Web Publishing Wizard (which is installed with the ValuPack)?

(•) No, I only want to publish objects locally.

( ) Yes, I want to run the Web Publishing Wizard to set up a new Web publishing specification.

( ) Yes, I want to use an existing Web Publishing server whose "friendly name" has been set up previously.

Friendly Name [▼]

All files in the folder you specify above will be sent to the server. Place your templates' supporting files there, such as .jpg or .gif files, and any .mdb file, so that the Web Publishing Wizard will send these to the server along with your Web publication.

| Cancel | < Back | Next > | Finish |

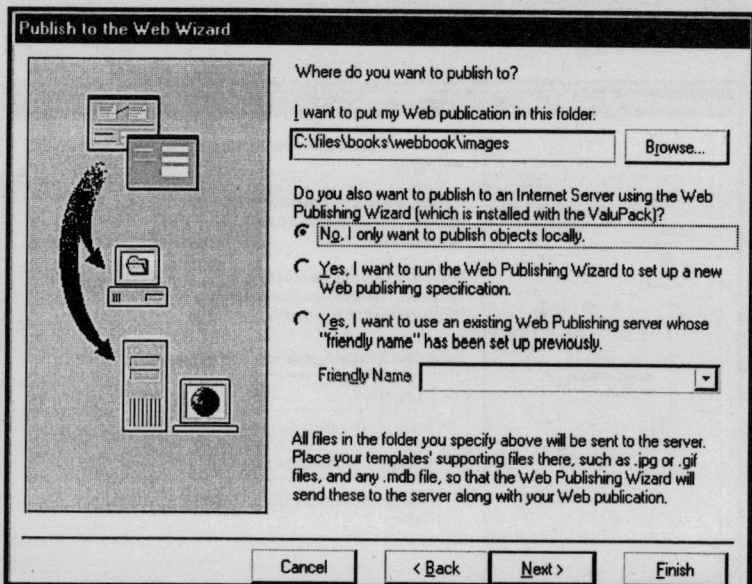

The next screen asks if want to create a home page (by ticking the box). You may also like to alter the name of your home page from Default to something more applicable.

The advantage of a home page is that it automatically structures your pages. You can always alter it afterwards.

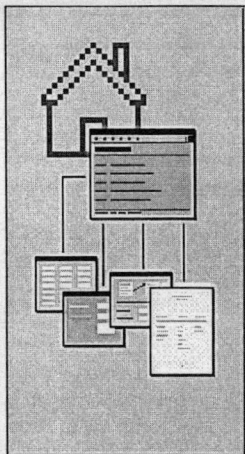

Publish to the Web Wizard

The wizard can create a home page for your Web publication. The home page includes a table with links to the published objects, so that all your Web pages are tied together.

☑ Yes, I want to create a home page.

What file name do you want for your home page?

home_page

| Cancel | < Back | Next > | Finish |

The next screen asks if you want to save the settings and choices you have made. This will speed up the process the next time you want to publish Access web pages.

If you then view your new home page in Explorer, it will look something like this.

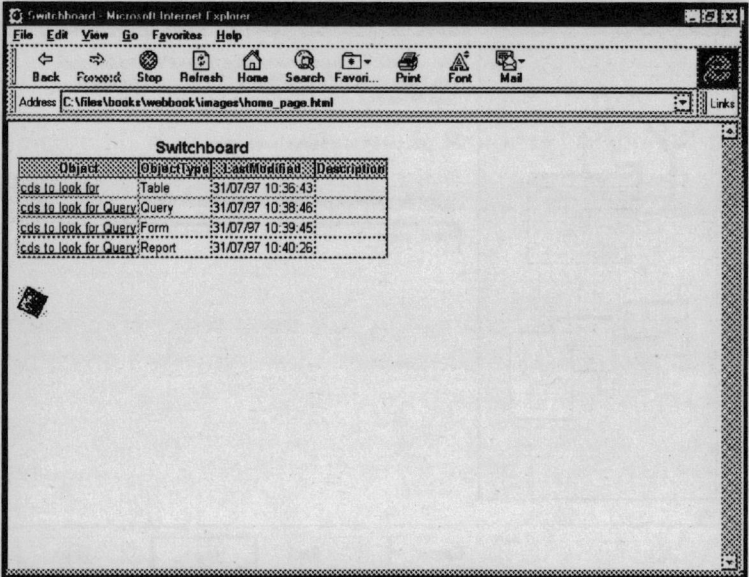

When you click on one of the links the browser will display the relevant page.

Add a hyperlink to a form, report, or datasheet

In Access, you can add clickable hypertext links within your Access file so the user can jump to another Access database, Word document, Excel worksheet or PowerPoint presentation on your Intranet or to any web page on any site anywhere.

You can store hyperlinks in fields in tables or as a label for a picture.

Creating a field to store hyperlinks

Open a table and make sure you are in **Design View**.

In the upper portion of the window, type in a field name for the field that you will use to store the hyperlinks. You may have to insert a new row if you are working with an existing table.

In the Data Type column for that field, select **Hyperlink**. Then switch back to **Datasheet View**. Now pull down the **Insert** menu and select **Hyperlink**.

You will see a dialog box in which you specify the page you wish to link to.

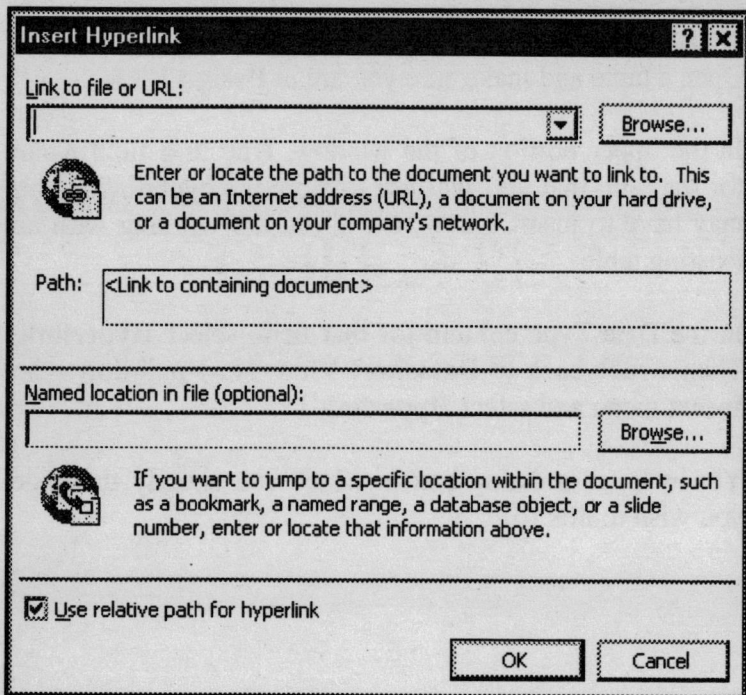

Insert Hyperlink

Link to file or URL:

Browse...

Enter or locate the path to the document you want to link to. This can be an Internet address (URL), a document on your hard drive, or a document on your company's network.

Path: <Link to containing document>

Named location in file (optional):

Browse...

If you want to jump to a specific location within the document, such as a bookmark, a named range, a database object, or a slide number, enter or locate that information above.

☑ Use relative path for hyperlink

OK   Cancel

Then save the table.

The link will be shown and if you click it, the browser will jump to the relevant page.

You can also **Insert** a link column in **Datasheet View** by pulling down the **Insert** menu and selecting **Hyperlink Column** and then **Inserting** the **Hyperlink** (however, you may want to alter the column name).

Pictures can also be made into links within an Access form.

MS Publisher

Web pages

MS Publisher is an excellent program to use for web page design because it allows you to create complex layouts and use pictures and text in innovative ways.

Be warned that this can lead to an over-exuberant approach and to a result that is unpleasant to view and is objectively poor in its ability to communicate.

To begin, from the initial screen after loading the program (or by pulling down the **File** menu and selecting **Create New Publication**), select **Blank Page** and then **Web Page**.

The screen will change to look like this.

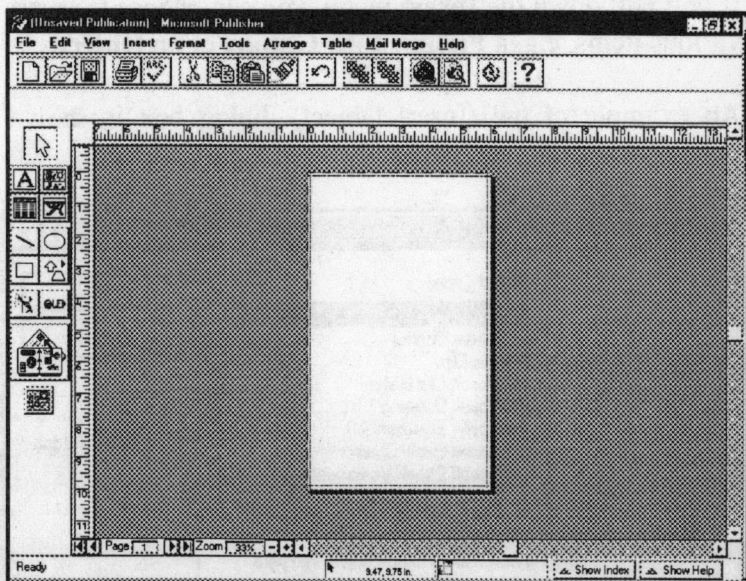

This is where you begin to create your web pages.

Entering text

Click on the **Text** button on the left of the screen, draw a rectangular shape (a text box), and type in the text.

You can format the text by using the commands in the **Format** menu (remember to highlight the text).

Entering objects

If you pull down the **Insert** menu, you can choose to insert various items, e.g. a **Picture File**, **Clipart** or an **Object**.

An example of the (Insert Object) dialog box is shown below.

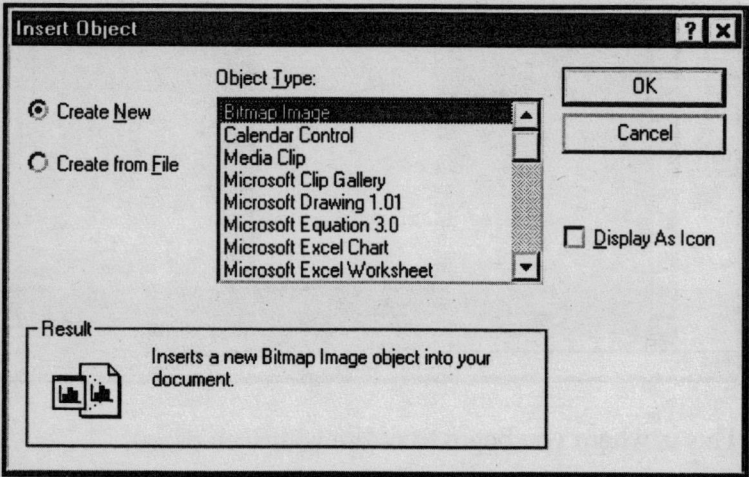

Once you have inserted the graphic, you can move it around the screen and format it (using the **Format** menu) to your desires (remember that to work with graphics you have to select them by clicking on them).

The pull down menus

This section looks at the features in the pull down menus that affect web page design.

This is **not** an exhaustive treatise on using MS Publisher (for that you need a book specific to the program itself) but an overview of the web specific features.

The File menu

Create New Publication...	Ctrl+N
Open Existing Publication...	Ctrl+O
Close Publication	
Save	Ctrl+S
Save As...	
Preview Web Site...	Ctrl+Shift+B
Web Site Properties...	
Publish to Web...	
Publish Web Site to Folder...	
Find File...	
Page Setup...	
Print Setup...	
Print...	Ctrl+P
1 C:\files\work\web\publisherpages	
Exit Publisher	Alt+F4

The commands of interest are shown in the middle of the pull down menu.

Preview Web Site

This loads your web browser and displays your page within the browser.

You can also access this by using the toolbar button.

Publish to Web

This was described within the chapter dealing with Word.

Web Site Properties

You can alter the properties of the web site you have created using MS Publisher. There should be no need to do so **unless** your IP requests you to when you upload the pages to your provider's site.

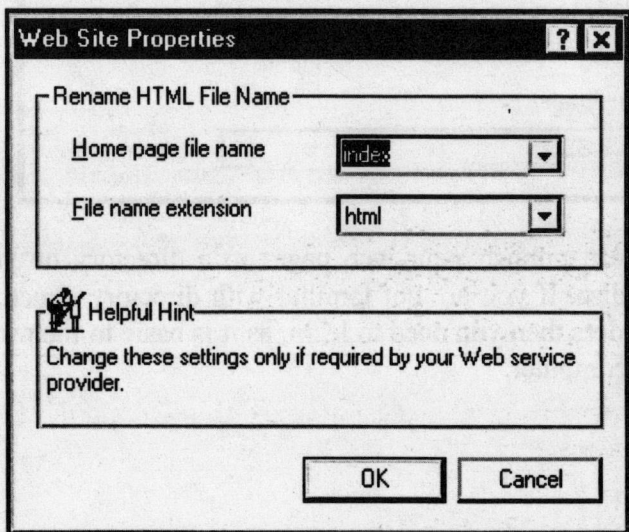

Publish Web Site to Folder

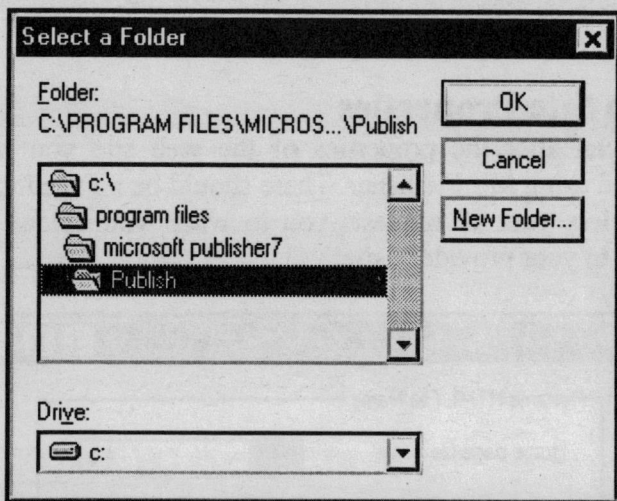

```
Select a Folder                                    [X]

Folder:                              ┌──────────────┐
C:\PROGRAM FILES\MICROS...\Publish    │      OK      │
                                     └──────────────┘
┌─────────────────────────────┐  ▲  ┌──────────────┐
│ 🗁 c:\                       │     │    Cancel    │
│   🗁 program files           │     └──────────────┘
│     🗁 microsoft publisher7  │     ┌──────────────┐
│       🗁 Publish             │     │  New Folder...│
│                             │     └──────────────┘
│                             │  ▼
└─────────────────────────────┘

Drive:
┌─────────────────────────────┐  ▼
│ 🖴 c:                        │
└─────────────────────────────┘
```

You can publish your web pages to a directory on your
hard disc. If you are not familiar with directory structures
or folders then you need to learn, as it is basic to the use of
your computer.

Format menu

There are various ways of altering the look and feel of your pages.

Background and Text Colors

If you choose the **Custom** option within the dialog box, you will be able to alter the colours of the hyperlinks. This is **not** necessarily a good idea, your readers may become confused.

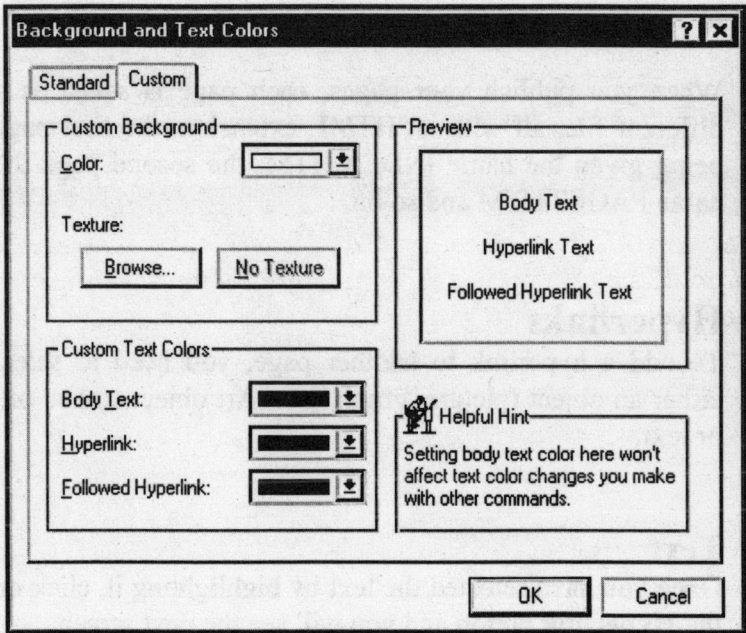

Background and Text Colors   ? ✕

| Standard | Custom |

Custom Background

Color: ⬚ ±

Texture:

Browse... No Texture

Custom Text Colors

Body Text: ▬ ±

Hyperlink: ▬ ±

Followed Hyperlink: ▬ ±

Preview

Body Text

Hyperlink Text

Followed Hyperlink Text

Helpful Hint

Setting body text color here won't affect text color changes you make with other commands.

OK   Cancel

You can, more productively, alter the background and body text colours. It is also possible to alter the pattern and texture of the page. Again, this may seem a good idea, however what looks good, initially, may be unreadable in reality. So, be careful.

Note that the changes affect all the pages produced.

Saving and publishing

When you save the file, it is stored with a PUB extension in whatever folder (directory) you choose.

When you publish your pages, each page is saved as a different file, all with an HTML extension, the first page being given the name INDEX.HTM, the second page the name PAGE2.HTM and so on.

Hyperlinks

To add a hyperlink to another page, you need to select either an object (picture, graph WordArt object and so on) or text.

Text

Once you have selected the text by highlighting it, click on the **Hyperlink** button and you will see the next screen.

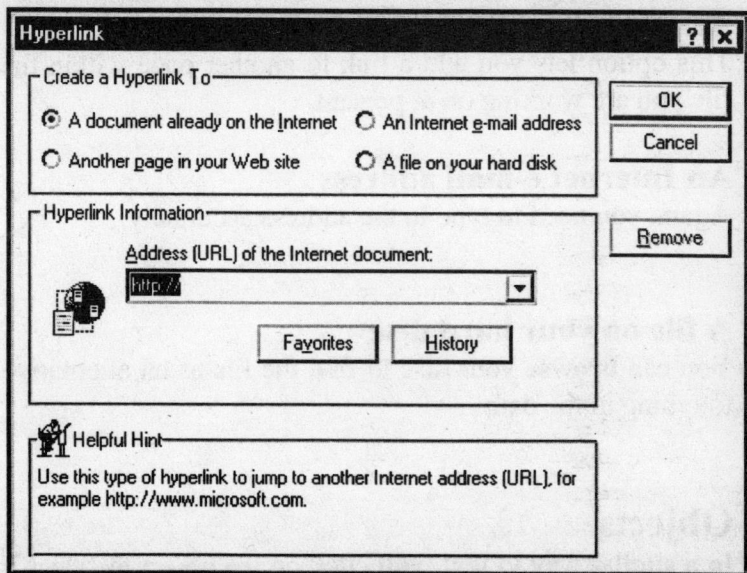

The data you need to enter will depend upon the choice you make in the top part of the dialog box (**Create a Hyperlink To**).

A document already on the Internet

You need to type in the URL (Internet address) of the page. It is **vital** to enter this exactly as URL's have to precise.

You may want to use the **History** and **Favorites** buttons to locate the address of a page you have looked at.

Another page on your web site

This option lets you add a link to another page within the file you are working on at present.

An Internet e-mail address

Again, you need to type in the address accurately.

A file on your hard disc

You can **browse** your disc to find the file as an alternative to typing in the path.

Objects

In a similar way to text, you click on the object to select it and then click on the **Hyperlink** button. The data you need to enter is described above (in the section dealing with text links).

Hotspots

When you use an image as a hyperlink then you can use different parts of the image as links to different web pages, i.e. you can divide the image into sections, each section linking to a different URL.

These sections are called **hotspots**.

To create a hotspot, click on the hotspot button
(left part of the screen below the other buttons).

Then simply draw a shape within the image (it has to be rectangular). The program then displays the dialog boxes to create the hyperlink as explained earlier.

Try to avoid overlapping the hotspot areas.

Writing HTML code

Introduction

Although you are likely to be creating your web pages using the main Office applications (Word, Excel, PowerPoint, Access or Publisher), it may be necessary to code manually at times. There are several reasons for this:

❑ You want to include certain techniques that are not available in the program you are using (for example if you are creating the pages using Word and you want to create frames within your web page).

❑ If you want to alter the page, you may find it easier to manipulate the code.

It is instructive, useful and intellectually satisfying to supplement your use of the application programs with a knowledge of coding.

The simplest way to begin this is to use Microsoft Explorer (and Notepad) as a vehicle either to write code from scratch or to alter existing code.

Fundamentals of HTML files

All HTML files follow a fixed structure.

When you use an application program such as Word, the structure is created for you, however you can type it in if you wish to create the whole file independently.

The structure is described below.

```
<html>

<head>
<title> an example of the use of html
</title>
</head>

<body>
the contents of your page
</body>

</html>
```

As you can see the structure is created by the use of **tags**, each tag begins a section of the file and there is a further tag (with a / symbol) to end that part of the structure.

The tags

<html></html>
The file begins and ends with this tag which defines it as an HTML file.

<head></head>
These tags contain the title and any other descriptive information you want to include in the file but not appear within the browser.

<title></title>
The descriptive title of your page is contained between these tags. Your choice of title is important, as it must give potential readers enough information about the contents.

The more descriptive a title is, the more likely you are to attract readers.

Titles are not displayed as part of your document, unless you deliberately include them (for example as a heading) but are often displayed in the title bar of a browser.

<body></body>
In this section, you enter the code to create your page.

A simple example

An example of the body text is shown below, which is followed by an explanation of the code.

```
<body>

<H1> david's first page</H1>
This makes use of <B>bold text</B>
<I>italic text</I>
<TT>typewriter style text</TT>

</body>
```

The tags can be capitalised or not as you prefer, although the trend is to capitalise.

<H1>

This is a first level heading, there are six heading levels (H1 to H6), H1 being the largest. Each level of heading has different formatting as well as being a different size and format. Two examples are shown below.

<H1> </H1>	1st level heading - large, bold (with automatic line breaks and spaces above and below the heading)
<H5> </H5>	5th level heading - small (line breaks, etc., as above)

\<B>\</B>

Any text contained within these tags will be in bold.

\<I>\</I>

Text between these tags will be in italic.

\<TT \</TT>

Use these if you want typewriter style text.

\<STRONG>\</STRONG>

Strong text (very similar to heading level 4) except that there is no additional line break as there is with headings.

You can combine tags.

Your first file

The methods I have found useful are as follows:

Creating a file from scratch

1. Load Windows Notepad.
2. Type in the basic structure for your file (see *Fundamentals*)
3. Save the file as an HTML file in whatever directory you wish (add an HTM extension to the file, i.e. **myfirstfile.htm**)
4. Close Notepad.
5. Load Microsoft Explorer.
6. Open the file you have just created.
7. Pull down the **View** menu and select **Source**.
8. This will re-open Notepad with the tags shown.
9. Enter the code you want in the **body** section of the file.
10. **Save** the file and switch back to Explorer.
11. Click on the **Refresh** button and you will see the results of your work within Explorer (as if you were viewing the page on the Internet).
12. When you want to make changes to the page, simply go back to step 7 and repeat steps 7 to 11 until happy.
13. Finally, close Notepad and Explorer.

This may seem a somewhat tortuous process but is actually quick and easy with practice.

Amending a file

Start at step 7 above.

Exercise One

Create a new file using Notepad. Type in the basic structure and then add the following body text. Call the file WEBONE.HTM

```
<h1>this is a level 1 heading</h1>
<h2>this is a level 2 heading</h2>
<h3>this is a level 3 heading</h3>
<h4>this is a level 4 heading</h4>
<h5>this is a level 5 heading</h5>
<h6>this is a level 6 heading</h6>
```

The results should look similar to this when viewed in the browser. There is a model answer shown on the next page.

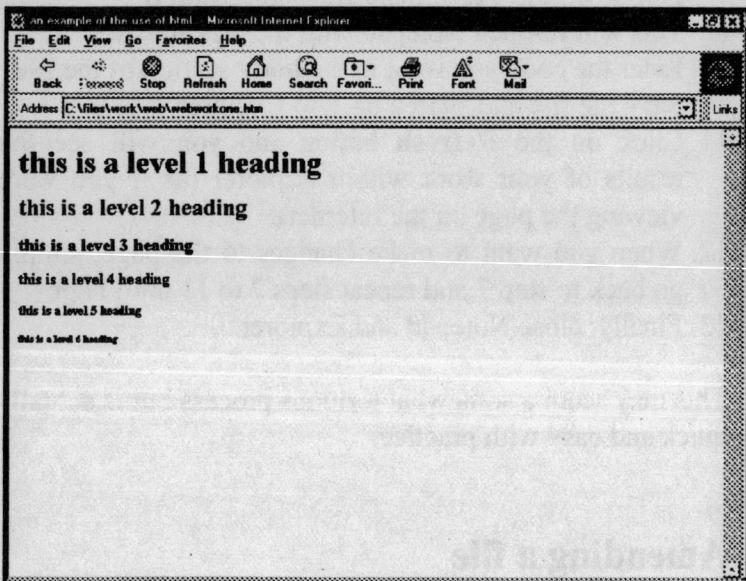

Model Answer to exercise one

```
<html>

<head>

<title> an example of the use of html </title>

</head>

<body>
<h1>this is a level 1 heading</h1>
<h2>this is a level 2 heading</h2>
<h3>this is a level 3 heading</h3>
<h4>this is a level 4 heading</h4>
<h5>this is a level 5 heading</h5>
<h6>this is a level 6 heading</h6>
</body>

</html>
```

Formatting tags

We have already looked at some of the formatting tags (bold, italic and so on). Here are some more for you to use (N means a number, zero to nine).

Remember the text to be formatted has to be included within the tags; (some) tags can be used in conjunction with each other.

You might like to create a new file and just experiment with these tags.

<U></U>
Underlining.

<PRE></PRE>
Pre-formatted text, any text within these tags will be laid out exactly as it appears within the tags. So, if you use tabs then these will be retained.

<CENTER></CENTER>
Centres the text within the tags, note the spelling.

<BLINK></BLINK>
The most mis-used tag in the language, avoid using this if possible, it makes text difficult and irritating to read. There are pages on the Net where the whole pages blinks on and off (usually combined with an unusual and vivid choice of colours). Note that this is a Netscape command and may (thankfully) not work within MS Explorer.

<FONT SIZE=NN></FONT>

The choice is from 1 (smallest) to 7 (largest). Unfortunately, whatever you choose may look larger or smaller when viewed if the reader is using a different screen resolution or has set their browser to different default settings.

<BASEFONT SIZE=NN>

This sets the default font size (from 1 to 7), the default, unless you alter it, is 3.

<FONT COLOR="#NNNNNN"></FONT>

You can alter the colour of the text, completely, words or single characters, by entering the hexadecimal code for the colour you want. To find the hexadecimal code, you can use a program such as Paint Shop Pro which can be set to display hexadecimal codes within the **Colour Pallet**.

There is a useful site that lists hex. codes at:

www.stardot.com/~lukeseem/hexed.html

<FONT COLOR="98C2F4">

This is a kind of bluish colour.

<FONT FACE="NAMEOFFONT"></FONT>

To alter the typeface of the text, insert a font name into the tag, e.g.

<FONT FACE="ARIAL">

Exercise Two

Create a new file called WEBTWO.HTM with the following body text and formatting.

I suggest you include the tag <P> to create a new paragraph between each section. This is a stand-alone tag which exists without the need to turn it off.

```
<body>

<U>Underlining</U>
<P>
<PRE>
        Pre-formatted text, any text within these
        tags will be laid out exactly as it appears
        within the tags. So if you use tabs then
        these will be retained.
</PRE>
<P>
<CENTER>Centres the text within the tags.</CENTER>
<P>
<FONT SIZE=1>The choice is from 1 (smallest)</FONT>
<P>
<FONT SIZE=7>The choice is from 7 (largest)</FONT>
<P>
<BASEFONT SIZE=5>This sets the default font size (from
1 to 7), the default, unless you alter it, is 3. This sets it to
5.
<P>
<FONT COLOR="98C2F4">This is a kind of bluish
colour.</FONT>
<P>
<FONT FACE="ARIAL">To alter the typeface of the text,
insert a font name into the tag, e.g. This is Arial</FONT>
</body>
```

134

This should look similar to the screen below.

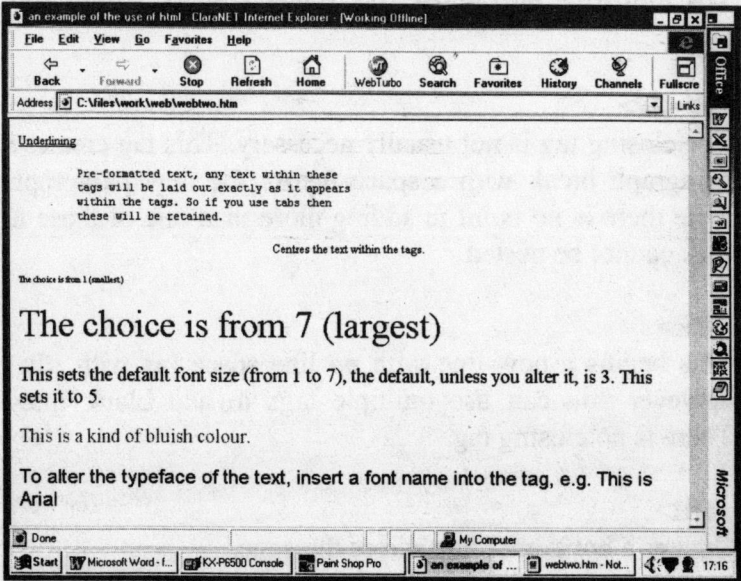

an example of the use of html - ClaraNET Internet Explorer - [Working Offline]

File   Edit   View   Go   Favorites   Help

Back   Forward   Stop   Refresh   Home   WebTurbo   Search   Favorites   History   Channels   Fullscre

Address   C:\files\work\web\webtwo.htm   Links

Underlining

        Pre-formatted text, any text within these
        tags will be laid out exactly as it appears
        within the tags. So if you use tabs then
        these will be retained.

                        Centres the text within the tags.

The choice is from 1 (smallest)

The choice is from 7 (largest)

This sets the default font size (from 1 to 7), the default, unless you alter it, is 3. This sets it to 5.

This is a kind of bluish colour.

To alter the typeface of the text, insert a font name into the tag, e.g. This is Arial

Done   My Computer

Start   Microsoft Word - f...   KX-P6500 Console   Paint Shop Pro   an example of ...   webtwo.htm - Not...   17:16

Ways of creating space(s)

The following tags allow you to create space within your page.

<P></P>
The closing tag is not usually necessary. This tag creates a paragraph break with a space *before* the new paragraph. Note there is no point in adding more than one of these as they cannot be nested.

**
**
This begins a new line with *no* line space (as with <P>) however you can use multiple tags to add blank lines. There is no closing tag.

<HR>
Creates a horizontal line across the page.

<HR SIZE=N><HR WIDTH=N> or <HR WIDTH=%>
Defines the size and width of the line in pixels (or width as a % of the page).

<HR NOSHADE>
Produces a solid line.

<P ALIGN=CENTER></P>
<HR ALIGN=RIGHT></HR>
<H3 ALIGN=LEFT></H3>
These commands align paragraphs <P ALIGN= >, or headings <H1 ALIGN= >, or horizontal rules (lines) <HR ALIGN= > and so on.

These tags can be combined if you wish.

Exercise three

Open your original file (WEBONE.HTM) in Explorer and add the following code (shown in bold) to experiment with space and horizontal lines to divide the page.

When you have saved the file as WEBTHREE.HTM, you will need to open the file in the browser.

Notice the different effects of using <P> and

```
<body>

<h1>this is a level 1 heading</h1>
<P>
<h2 ALIGN=RIGHT>this is a level 2 heading</h2>

<h3>this is a level 3 heading</h3>
<HR NOSHADE SIZE=50 width=50%>
<h4>this is a level 4 heading</h4>
<BR>
<h5 ALIGN=CENTER>this is a level 5 heading</h5>
<BR>
<BR>
<BR>
<HR SIZE=20 width=100%>
<h6>this is a level 6 heading</h6>

</body>
```

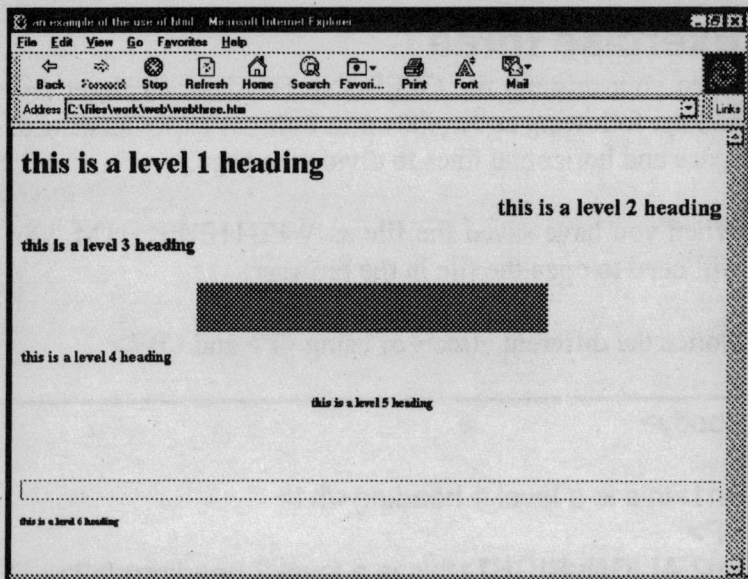

Exercise four

This exercise explores the code you have learnt so far and begins to build up your own home page.

Create a new file, called MYPAGE.HTM and enter your own details using the formatting shown (below) in bold. Enter paragraph or break tags as necessary.

title
my first home page

body

Change the font, the colour (e2380 is the hex code for red), centre this heading and make it heading level 2
Your name's home page

Heading level 4, in red and centred
created on date

Put in a horizontal line, size 10 pixels, no shading and 30% width of the page

heading level 4, colour red
address
revert to normal (default) text
type in your address
there should be a new line
for each part of the address
heading level 4, colour red
e-mail
revert to normal (default) text
type in your e-mail address
if you do not have one then type the following
strong text in italic
your E-mail address
heading level 4, colour red
occupation
revert to normal (default) text
type in your job title
endbody

Your page may look similar to this although please experiment.

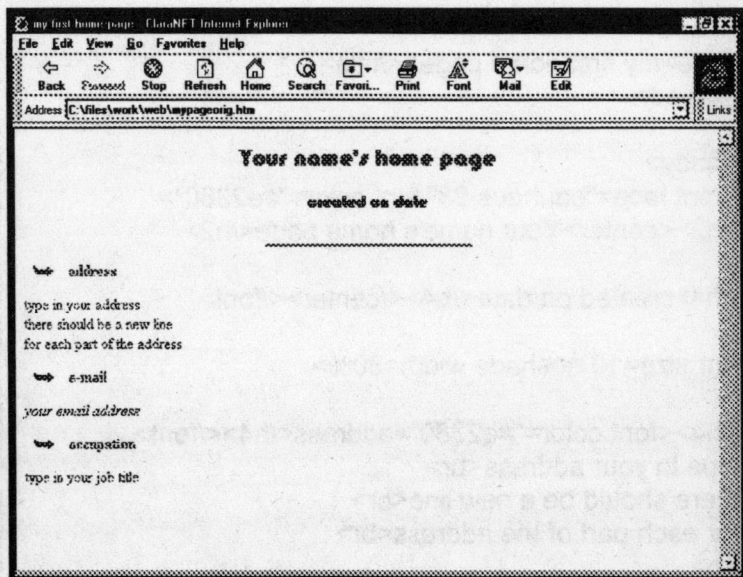

The coding for the page shown above is as follows

```
<html>
<head>
<title>my first home page></title>
</head>

<body>
<font face="bauhaus 93" font color="#e2380">
<h2><center>Your name's home page</h2>

<h4>created on date</h4></center></font>

<hr size=10 noshade width=30%>

<h4><font color="#e2380">address</h4></font>
type in your address<br>
there should be a new line<br>
for each part of the address<br>
<p>
<br>

<h4><font color="#e2380">e-mail</h4></font>
<strong><i>your E-mail address </i></strong>
<br>
<p>
<br>

<h4><font color="#e2380">occupation</h4></font>
type in your job title
</body>

</html>
```

Background colours

You have already looked at the coding for text colours, it is just as easy to alter the background. The tags are described below.

<BODY BACKGROUND="FILE">
This uses a picture file as the background, think **very** carefully before doing this as it can lead to difficulty in reading the text. The file should be in a GIF format and stored in the same directory as the page.

<BODY BGCOLOR="#NNNNNN">
To alter the background colour from white, again consider legibility.

<BODY TEXT="#NNNNNN">
This alters the body text colour, you use this for all the text and then <FONT COLOR=> to alter the colour of individual words.

Exercise five

Open the file MYPAGE.HTM and alter the body text colour to a kind of green (hex:4125346) and the background to light yellow (hex:f2f4c6). Note how the headings remain in red (the colours may display differently on your v.d.u.)

Adding graphics to your pages

Most browsers will display graphics and if the reader has a multi-media system, they can view movie clips and sounds as well.

You can include any graphic you wish, a company logo or a scanned picture of you and your family or employees (or better still a digitised photograph).

Always remember that the reader may be using a text only browser or may have turned off the graphics so that the pages load more quickly (this is a common trick when the Internet is busy). You must ensure that your pages are at the very least understandable and possibly optimised for text only browsers (depending upon your projected client audience).

The code for adding a graphic is:

<IMG SRC="image.gif">

An important aspect of graphics is that they have to be in certain file formats i.e. .GIF or .JPEG. You will have to convert your file to one of these formats using a program such as Paint Shop Pro.

Positioning graphics

You have some control over the position of the graphics on your pages. **The tags align the text to the image** (not to the page as in <CENTER>).

ALIGN=TOP (or BOTTOM or MIDDLE)

This code is included within the IMG tag, i.e.

<IMG SRC="IMAGE.GIF" ALIGN=RIGHT>

The effect of the tag will depend upon whether the text is before or after the image in your coding.

For text only browsers, you should include some code to display text instead of a picture for those benighted souls using out of date browsers.

<IMG SRC="IMAGE.GIF" ALT="the picture shows an image of a cat">

The ALT tag adds text, which is displayed instead of the image for text only browsers.

Image dimensions, space and borders

The following tags define (in pixels) the size of the image on your page, the white space around the image and put a border (size in pixels) around the image.

The number of pixels on the screen is determined by the resolution of your screen, thus if you are using 640 x 480 resolution, this is the number of pixels on the screen.

WIDTH=NN HEIGHT=NN (can also be a % of screen)
BORDER=NN (this may only work in Netscape)
SPACE=NN VSPACE=NN

An example:

<IMG SRC="IMAGE.GIF" WIDTH=200 HEIGHT=300>

Exercise six

Find an image you like and convert it into GIF format.

Add this to your own home page MYPAGE.HTM, adding the code to the line beneath the first heading on your page (Your name home page) and format it as follows:

- Create a border of 5 pixels (Netscape only)
- Size the image: width 10% and height 15%
- Put 5 pixels of white space around the image

Now align the image to the right

Once you have the general idea, it is time to experiment.

- Move (cut and paste) the line of code for the image before the second line of your address and align to top, you will see the effect changes dramatically.

- Now alter the white space to 20 pixels and again the effect changes.

- Alter the vertical space (VSPACE) measurement to zero and yet again look at the changes.

- Alter the horizontal rule size to 3.

- Write the following code after the initial headings but before the horizontal line (this will change the spacing slightly so the page should fit onto the screen; however this will depend on the resolution your screen is set to): </FONT><FONT SIZE=1>

At this point, your page should resemble that shown below.

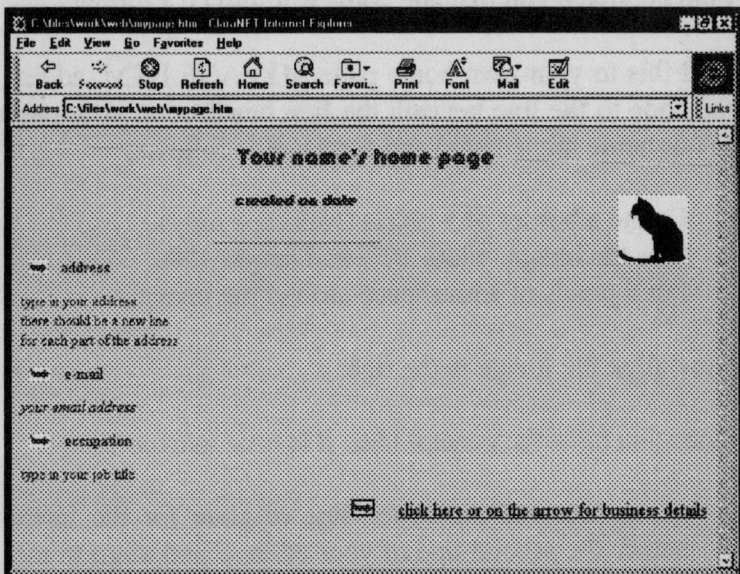

C:\files\work\web\mypage.htm - ClaraNET Internet Explorer

File   Edit   View   Go   Favorites   Help

Back   ....   Stop   Refresh   Home   Search   Favori...   Print   Font   Mail   Edit

Address   C:\files\work\web\mypage.htm   Links

Your name's home page

created on date

➤ address

type in your address
there should be a new line
for each part of the address

➤ e-mail

your email address

➤ occupation

type in your job title

✉ click here or on the arrow for business details

Model answer for exercise six

```
<HTML>

<HEAD>

<TITLE>my first home page</TITLE>

</HEAD>

<BODY          TEXT="#800080"          LINK="#0000ff"
VLINK="#800080" BGCOLOR="#f2f4c6">

<FONT  FACE="Bauhaus  93"  COLOR="#ff0000"><H2
ALIGN="CENTER">Your name's home page</H2>
<IMG  SRC="file:///c:/files/work/web/cat.gif"  ALIGN="right"
WIDTH=10%   HEIGHT=15%   VSPACE=0   HSPACE=20
BORDER=5>
<H4 ALIGN="CENTER">created on date</H4>

</FONT><FONT SIZE=1></font>

<P><HR WIDTH="30%" SIZE=1 noshade></P>


<FONT COLOR="#ff0000"><H4>
<IMG  SRC="ARROW.gif"  ALIGN=middle      WIDTH=3%
HEIGHT=3% VSPACE=0 HSPACE=10>
address</FONT>
</H4><nobr>
type in your address<BR>
there should be a new line<BR>
for each part of the address

<FONT COLOR="#ff0000">
```

```
<H4><IMG          SRC="ARROW.gif"          ALIGN=middle
WIDTH=3% HEIGHT=3% VSPACE=0 HSPACE=10>
e-mail</H4>

</FONT><I>your E-mail address</I>

<FONT                    COLOR="#ff0000"><H4><IMG
SRC="ARROW.gif" ALIGN=middle
WIDTH=3%           HEIGHT=3%           VSPACE=0
HSPACE=10>occupation</H4>
</font>type in your job title <p align=right>
<font    size=4    font    face="times    new    roman"><a
href="pagetwo.htm"><img    src="arrow.gif"    hspace=20
width=3%  height=3%>click  here  or  on  the  arrow  for
business details</A>

</BODY>

</HTML>
```

Exercise seven

Using the same file, move the line of code (for the image) back between the first heading and the second heading and align it to the right.

❑ Now add an (arrow) graphic to your file. Format this as shown below and place the code for the graphic **after** each of the <H4> tags for the address, e-mail and occupation headings
❑ Align it to the middle
❑ Width and height should be 3%
❑ Vertical space is zero and horizontal space is 10 pixels
❑ No border
❑ Add multiple <BR> to space out the text

Your page should now look like this.

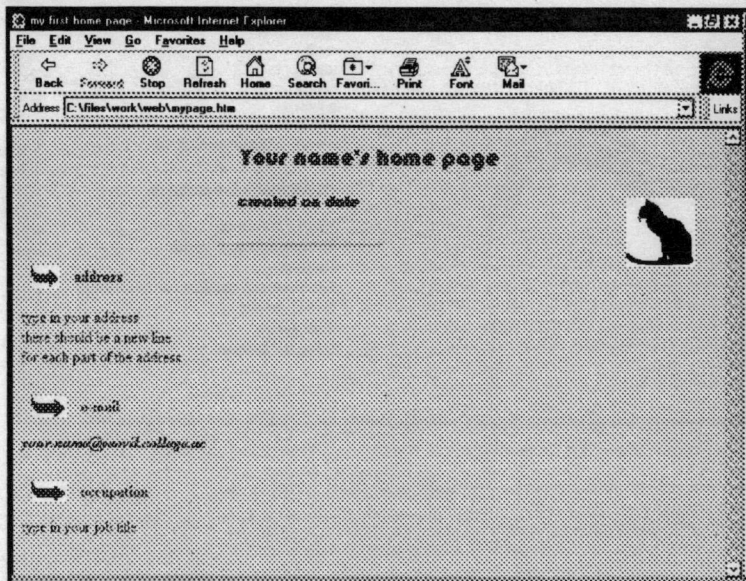

Exercise eight

The next step is to produce another page, which you can call PAGETWO.HTM

This should contain a logo for your business and details of the business address, telephone, e-mail, a synopsis of its business activities and a contact name.

Lay this out as you wish using the tags that have been covered so far (N.B. you do **not** need to use all of them).

My page is shown below:

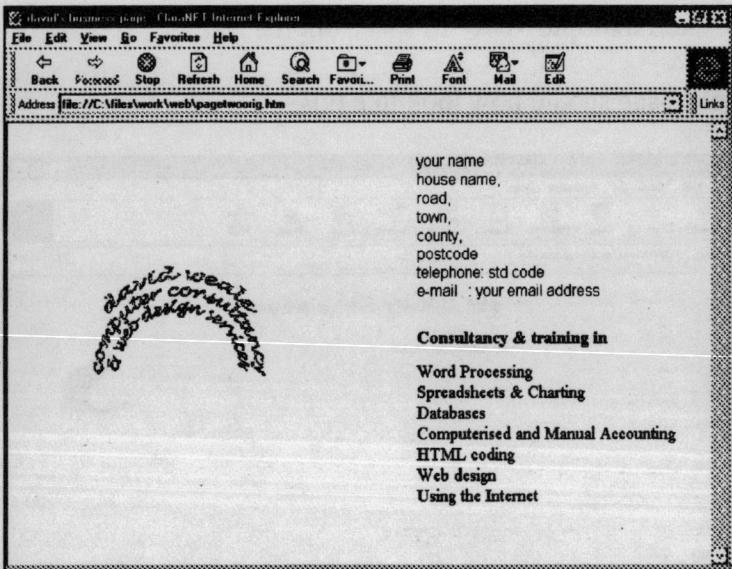

Model answer to exercise eight

```html
<html>
<head>
<title>
david's business page</title>
</head>

<body>
<font size=4>
<img  src="logo.gif"  align=left  height=25%  width=25%
vspace=130 hspace=80>
<pre><font face="arial">
david weale f.c.a.
house name,
road,
town,
county,
postcode
telephone: std code
e-mail   : your E-mail address</pre><br>
<font face="times new roman">
<h3>Consultancy & training in</h3>
Word Processing<br>
Spreadsheets & Charting<br>
Databases<br>
Computerised and Manual Accounting<br>
HTML coding<br>
Web design<br>
Using the Internet<br><p>
</font>
<font size=4 font face="times new roman">

</body>
</html>
```

Linking pages

One of the fundamentals of the Internet is the use of hypertext links. This makes it easy to move from one page to another (or within a page itself).

Normally links are underlined and in blue. You can create text links and / or graphics links to other pages (these links can be to another of your pages or to pages on another site).

Text links

The coding for these is:

<A HREF="URL">text explaining the link**</A>**

The **A** stands for an anchor and is an integral part of the syntax. The URL is the address of the file you are linking to (whether on your hard disc or on the Internet.

Please remember to include some text otherwise you will have a link but nothing will appear on the page.

E-mail links

If you want the reader to email you, you have to use a special hypertext link:

<A HREF=MAILTO:YOUR_EMAIL_ADDRESS>anytext</A>

This has not been included in the model answers as clicking on the link will load your mail program.

Exercise nine

Now to link your two pages together. Start with MYPAGE.HTM and place the link at the bottom of the page. The URL will be the address of your second file PAGETWO.HTM

Then open PAGETWO.HTM and insert a link at the bottom of that page back to the first file.

You can alter the font sizes and so on to ensure that the pages fit on one screen.

When you browse either of these files, you should be able to click on the link and go directly to the other page. If this happens you have been successful.

Graphics links

To use graphics as a link simply include a reference to the graphic within the hypertext code, i.e.

<A HREF="MYPAGE.HTM"> <IMG SRC="ARROW.GIF">
click here or on the arrow to move to the business page </A>

The graphic links may be bordered in blue to show that they are links and a hand will appear when you move the mouse over them (the same as with text links).

It is possible to have purely graphics links although this might just confuse the reader, unless the graphic also contains text.

Exercise ten

Add the above line to your file PAGETWO.GIF (at the bottom) and then do the same for the other file.

Below is an example of how the second page could look.

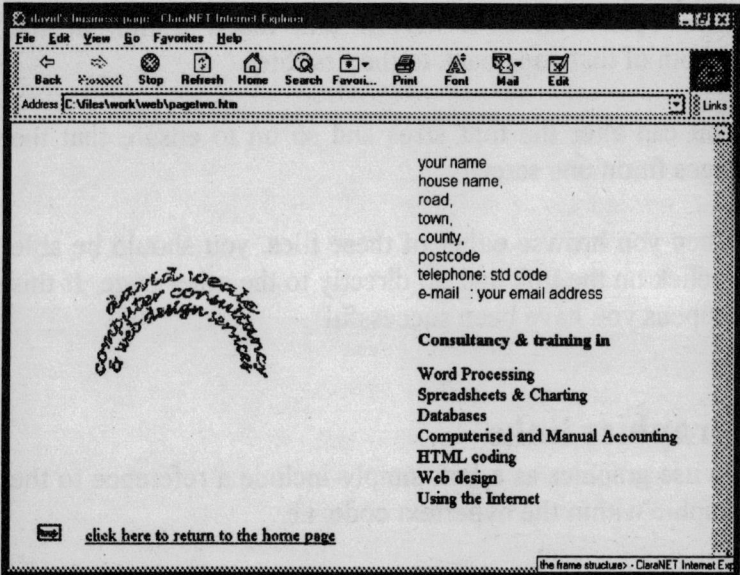

Model answer for exercise ten

```
<html>
<head>
<title>
david's business page</title>
</head>
<body>
<font size=4>
<img  src="logo.gif"  align=left  height=25%  width=25%
vspace=130 hspace=80>
<pre><font face="arial">
david weale f.c.a.
house name,
road,
town,
county,
postcode
telephone: std code
e-mail  to your E-mail address</pre><br>
<font face="times new roman">
<h3>Consultancy & training in</h3>
Word Processing<br>
Spreadsheets & Charting<br>
Databases<br>
Computerised and Manual Accounting<br>
HTML coding<br>
Web design<br>
Using the Internet<br><p></font>
<font  size=4  font  face="times  new  roman"><A
HREF="MYPAGE.HTM"><img src="arrow.gif" hspace=20
width=3%  height=3%>click  here  to  return  to  the  home
page</A>
</body>
</html>
```

Lists

You may want to create lists of items.

Unordered lists

Unordered lists display bullets on each line of the list.

The code for these is:

```
<UL>
<LI>
</UL>
```

The <L1> tag must appear before every item in the list

If you want to introduce different style of bullets then

<UL TYPE="SQUARE" or "DISC" or "CIRCLE">

will produce square or disc bullets instead of round ones (though not necessarily in all browsers).

Ordered lists

Ordered lists are numbered lists

```
<OL>
<LI>
</OL>
```

Nested lists

You can have lists within lists if you so wish (both numbered and bulleted lists).

```
<ul TYPE="CIRCLE">
<li>this is a list of music I like
<li>billie holiday
<li>t-bone walker
<li>big joe turner
<li>jimmy rushing

<ul>
<li>a nested lists begins here of other musicians
<li>louis jordan
<li>etta james
<li>ray charles
</ul>
</ul>
```

To begin a nested list simply start with another <UL> or <OL> **without** closing the original list.

Be careful to (eventually) close the list with the closing tag </UL> or </OL> and enter this tag as many times as there are nests.

There are various changes you can make to numbered (ordered) lists.

Changing the numbering of ordered lists

<OL START=N>
Changes the start number for the list

<LI VALUE=N>
Alters the number from that line

<OL TYPE=i>
Produces roman numeral type numbers. Also I, a, A can be used.

Be careful here, you may need to include a tag in the nested list to define the start number (the value is a number, whatever format your are using), e.g.
<LI VALUE=6>

Using lists for links
You can create a list for your links if you want.

<OL>
<LI><A   HREF="http://www.yeovil.ac.uk>Visit   the Yeovil College site**</A>**
etc.
</OL>

Below is an example of lists (the code was described earlier).

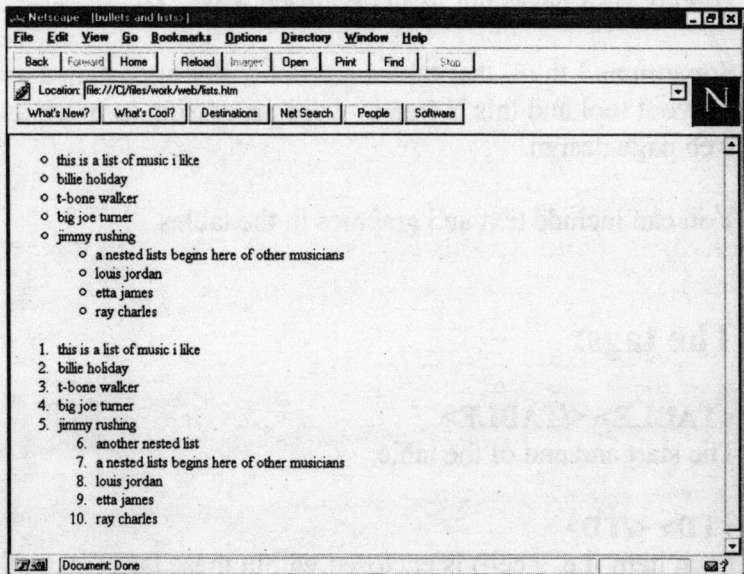

Exercise eleven

Create a file containing **both** an unordered (bulleted) list and an ordered (numbered) list. Ensure that you have included nested lists for both. The content of the lists can be anything you wish (if you have no ideas, perhaps you could produce a list similar to mine).

Tables

Very, very, useful and worth persevering with as they let you lay your pages out in an organised way.

Sometimes I think that tables are not really appreciated as a layout tool and this is true in word processing as much as web page design.

You can include text and graphics in the tables.

The tags:

<TABLE> </TABLE>
The start and end of the table.

<TD> </TD>
Each item (i.e. a cell) is enclosed within these tags (each of these defines the column).

<TR> </TR>
Defines a row.

You begin with a row, entering the data for that row, then close that row and begin on the next row and so on.

Table borders

To make your table look impressive, you can add formatting.

These are included within the <TABLE> tag.

BORDER=N (pixels)
CELLSPACING=N
CELLPADDING=N

An example of the coding and the subsequent table are shown below.

```
<body>
<h4>this is a table !</h4>

<table border=15 cellspacing=15 cellpadding=5>

<tr>
<td>row one, column one of the table</td>
<td>column two</td>
<td>column three</td>
</tr>

<tr>
<td>row two, column one of the table</td>
<td>column two</td>
<td>column three</td>
</tr>

</table>

</body>
```

Additional table tags

Table captions
If you want to include a caption explaining the table, use the following tags.

<CAPTION> text </CAPTION>

You can alter the font and so on by adding the necessary code, e.g.

<CAPTION FONT SIZE=5>

Table headings
Similar to the <TD> tag but the text is in bold and centred. The tags are:

<TH> </TH>

Aligning text in tables
You can align text using the following additional code.

ALIGN=LEFT or CENTER or RIGHT

VALIGN=TOP or MIDDLE or BOTTOM

ALIGN aligns text horizontally, VALIGN aligns vertically within the cells.

COLSPAN=2

This merges two rows into one.

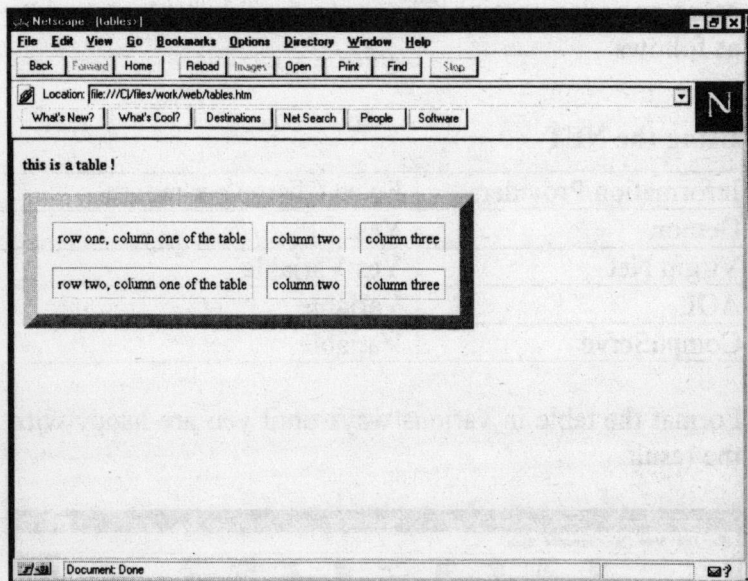

Instead of text, you can include a link or a graphic.

Exercise twelve

Create a file containing a table of five rows and two columns with a caption. The contents of the table should be as follows:

Using the NET

Information Providers	Fixed Charge per month
Demon	Yes
Virgin Net	Yes/Variable
AOL	Variable
CompuServe	Variable

Format the table in various ways until you are happy with the result.

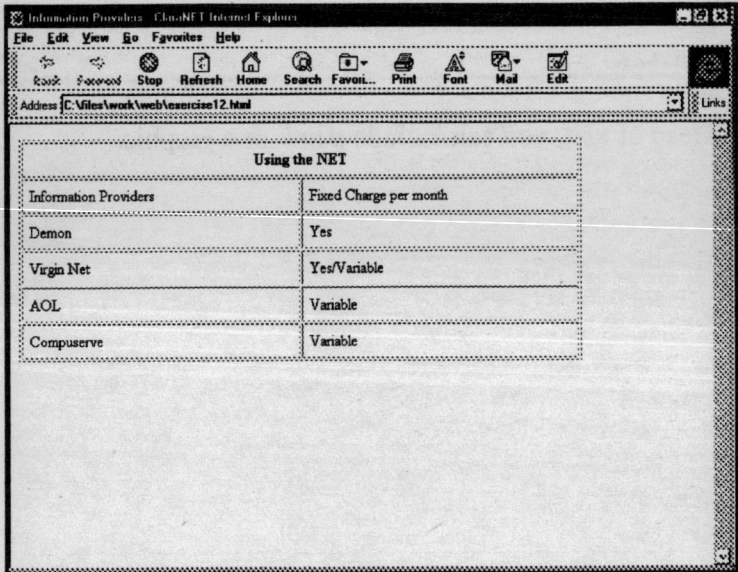

Model answer to exercise twelve

```
<HTML>
<HEAD>
<TITLE>Information Providers</TITLE>
</HEAD>
<TABLE BORDER CELLSPACING=2 CELLPADDING=7
WIDTH=590>
<TR><TD VALIGN="MIDDLE" COLSPAN=2>
<B><P ALIGN="CENTER">Using the NET</B></TD>
</TR>
<TR><TD WIDTH="50%" VALIGN="TOP">
<P>Information Providers</TD>
<TD WIDTH="50%" VALIGN="TOP">
<P>Fixed Charge per month</TD></TR>
<TR><TD WIDTH="50%" VALIGN="TOP">
<P>Demon</TD>
<TD WIDTH="50%" VALIGN="TOP">
<P>Yes</TD></TR>
<TR><TD WIDTH="50%" VALIGN="TOP">
<P>Virgin Net</TD>
<TD WIDTH="50%" VALIGN="TOP">
<P>Yes/Variable</TD></TR>
<TR><TD WIDTH="50%" VALIGN="TOP">
<P>AOL</TD>
<TD WIDTH="50%" VALIGN="TOP">
<P>Variable</TD></TR>
<TR><TD WIDTH="50%" VALIGN="TOP">
<P>Compuserve</TD>
<TD WIDTH="50%" VALIGN="TOP">
<P>Variable</TD></TR>
</TABLE>
</BODY>
</HTML>
```

Frames

Frames divide the page into separate sections and you add the content to the frames. You can link (with hypertext links) one frame to another if you wish although this is optional and you may want to just use frames to divide the page rather than provide a more sophisticated approach.

I suggest you look at pages on the Net using frames to get an idea of structure, layout and so on, this is especially important with frames as there are some very sophisticated but fairly useless pages out there where technique has won over readability. View the source code to see how the page was constructed.

The tags for frames

<FRAMESET ROWS/COLS=N,N> </FRAMESET>
Start and end of the frame.

N is a numeric value and can be:
- [ ] fixed (number of pixels) or
- [ ] % of screen or
- [ ] N,* relative to remainder of windows (e.g. 200 then the second value is the remainder of space) or
- [ ] *,2* (this means the second value is twice the size of the first)

\<FRAME SRC=contents\>
The contents will be a web page.

\<FRAME SRC=file.htm NAME=name_of_frame\>
If you name a frame then it can be used as a target (i.e. you can display files within that frame by calling it from another frame - see illustrated code later) .

\<NORESIZE\>
Fixes the size of the frame

\<SCROLLING=yes/no/auto\>
You can have scrollbars or not or leave it to the system to decide

These tags can be combined, e.g.

\<FRAME SRC=file.htm NORESIZE SCROLLING=NO\>

\<NOFRAMES\>
This is useful to put inside the \<FRAMESET\> tag so that browsers can be used that do not accept frames

If you want to design your pages to be reasonably acceptable to (noframe) browsers, keep the design simple as it is difficult to design good pages for both frames and noframes.

Links within frames

<A HREF="url" TARGET=WWWWW>

The TARGET can be:
_self (within the same frame)

_parent (replaces the current contents with that in the <A HREF=>)

Examples

<A HREF=one.htm TARGET=NEWFRAME>
This replaces the ONE.HTM page with that in the NEWFRAME

<A HREF=one.htm TARGET=_parent>
Replaces the current contents with ONE.HTM

A real life example

When you are doing this yourself, it is necessary to be very precise about the structure. I suggest you write down the way in which the files interact, so that you are clear about what you are trying to do and how you intend to achieve it.

The files

The initial file containing the frame structure

```
<HTML>
<head>
<title>the frame structure></title>
</head>

<body>
<frameset cols=30%,*>
<frame src=frames2.htm name=frames1>
<frame src=logo.gif name=frames2>
</frameset>
</body>

</HTML>
```

The file containing the contents of the frames

```
<HTML>
<head>
<title>the frame structure</title>
</head>

<body>
<h2>contents</h2>
<ul>
<li><a href=mypage.htm target=frames2><h4>my home
page</a>
<li><a        href=pagetwo.htm        target=frames2>second
page</h4></a>
</ul>
</body>

</HTML>
```

Exercise thirteen

Type in these files, naming them FRAMES1.HTM and
FRAMES2.HTM and see how they work. Adjust the code
to personalise it (after getting it to work).

The illustrations are of the original content page and the
screen after clicking on the first item in the contents (my
home page)

I have used files which already exist (you have created
these yourself).

Browser window 1:

the frame structure - Microsoft Internet Explorer

File   Edit   View   Go   Favorites   Help

Back   Forward   Stop   Refresh   Home   Search   Favori...   Print   Font   Mail

Address C:\files\work\web\frames1.htm

contents

- my home page
- second page

david weale computer consultancy & web design services

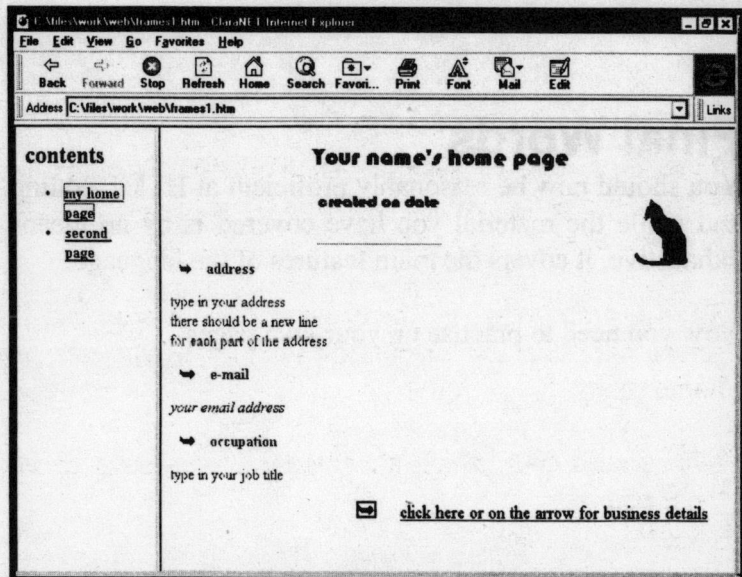

Browser window 2:

C:\files\work\web\frames1.htm - ClaraNET Internet Explorer

File   Edit   View   Go   Favorites   Help

Back   Forward   Stop   Refresh   Home   Search   Favori...   Print   Font   Mail   Edit

Address C:\files\work\web\frames1.htm

contents

- my home page
- second page

Your name's home page

created on date

➡ address

type in your address
there should be a new line
for each part of the address

➡ e-mail

your email address

➡ occupation

type in your job title

✉ click here or on the arrow for business details

More information

The Internet is full of information about itself and HTML coding is no exception. The language is changing rapidly with new tags and techniques (extensions) being added.

Each new version of the browsers introduces new features to keep that browser ahead. The other browser(s) then incorporate those new features and so the language grows.

The following links may be of assistance (note that URL's do disappear sometimes or the pages are hosted on a different site and so on). There are many other textbooks and help on the Net.

http://werbach.com/barebones/
www.cs.indiana.edu/docproject/zen/
www.projectcool.com/developer/

Final Words

You should now be reasonably proficient at HTML coding and while the material you have covered is by no means exhaustive, it covers the main features of the language.

Now you need to practise on your own pages.

Designing web pages

First thoughts

Decide upon what you are trying to achieve.

Look at other sites, especially your competitors.

Plan who you are targeting and how will you attract this target group.

Getting readers for your site

Include your URL in all company literature (letters, invoices, advertising, etc.).

Include the web site address in **all** company literature (in-house and external).

Maintain the site by checking the contents regularly and update the information **and links** (out of date information is a quick way to kill interest in a site), to make your site interesting, add new material regularly.

Use forms and/or counters to analyse the response to the site

Include your E-mail address and if you are expecting a response from abroad remember to include your international dialling code for telephone or fax replies.

Advertising your site

Get your site included in as many search engines as possible. Useful addresses for this are:

www.yahoo.com/
www.yell.co.uk

www.qwiklaunch.com	(notifies the 15 leading engines for you)
www.linkexchange.com/	(enables your banner to be advertised, free in 50,000 other pages.

General design tips

Write concisely, clearly, and **simply**.

Always test your pages exhaustively for sense, spelling, grammar, layout and links.

Try to avoid using HTML code that is specific to any one browser (although Netscape and Microsoft appear to be agreeing a standard language).

The <title> will be used as a bookmark so make sure that your title is descriptive of the contents.

Copyright applies to web pages as much as it does to printed material (as do the laws of defamation and so on).

If you leave the most important material to the end of the page there is a possibility that the reader will not get that far.

Try to avoid the need for the reader to scroll (better to start a new page using hypertext links from one to the other or use links within the page or frames).

Backgrounds

Be very careful if you want to use textured or coloured backgrounds to your pages, they can make the text more difficult to read. There are some subtle backgrounds available from:

www.sfsu.edu/~jtolson/textures/textures.htm

Links

Links should contain a description explaining why the viewer may want to look at them.

Use standard colours for links, otherwise it can be confusing for the reader.

Make it obvious what text and pictures are links so that the reader is clear where to click the mouse.

Text

Black text on a white background is traditional (after all this is how books have been produced for centuries), if you feel this is too boring then try dark colours on a light background and so on. If you reverse the colours (e.g. white text on a black background) then you may it difficult to read and to print on paper.

Unfortunately, colours that look good on your (state of the art) v.d.u. may look terrible on cheap monitors so be careful.

Blinking text (or pages) is bad news and scrolling text (marquees) and animations can become tiresome quickly and may not display properly in all browsers or screens.

Experiment but always test new ideas with a sample of your intended audience.

Some users may have larger (or smaller) monitors, consider this when choosing the smallest font size you intend to use.

Images

Consider using thumbnails and allowing the viewer to download the full image if they want to (include a file size indicator).

Minimising the file size

You need to experiment to get the best balance between image filesize (and consequent download time) and quality of image. You can alter the resolution, number of colours or file type to get the best compromise.

Never assume that your readers are using a visual browser (even if they have a state of the art browser they may have turned off the images for speed), always use an <IMG ALT="text"> so that the reader knows what they are missing.

Speed

Remember that large files take time to download and the viewer can get irritated quickly (especially if they are paying the telephone bills).

Try to avoid long download times as the viewer may click the **STOP** button. Large graphics can slow the download times.

It is recommended that the initial page should download quickly (less than 10-15 seconds at average download speeds)

Reverse engineering

Spend some time looking around the Net at the way in which pages and sites are constructed. You will learn much, some good, some bad. I suggest you look at the source code of the pages you find attractive. There is nothing wrong with adapting other people's ideas, this is very different from plagiarism.

Remember there are very few geniuses, most of us make do with a little inspiration and a lot of hard work.

Site Structure

Divide your site into a series of pages, each with a link to the (next and previous) and organise them in a coherent and logical way. It is best to put a NEXT button (a hypertext link to the next page) at the end of every page (except the last!), a PREVIOUS button and a HOME button.

Each page should be independent of the others (and contain links to your home page) since the user may have jumped to a page on your site that is not your home page.

Saving the pages

As you are constructing a series of pages and each is a separate HTML file then you may want to keep them all together in the same directory or you may want to create a directory structure to mirror the structure of the pages.

Will your pages be found?

Submit your URL (Internet address) to the major search engines and directories. You need only submit the first or index page and the search engines will follow the links to the remainder of your pages indexing as they go.

Your Information provider may submit your pages to the major search engines for you.

There will be a time delay between submitting your URL and your pages being indexed, this can be several weeks so be patient.

A useful site giving details is: (this site also includes a list of sites that will submit your pages for you free):

http://www.fingertek.com/submit.htm

Search engines do not always index the same type of material, for example, some index the contents of META tags and others do not.

Search engines index keywords so it is best to make sure that you include descriptions and keywords in the following parts of your pages.

META tags
Title
Contents (body text)

Both the META tags and the TITLE tags are included within the HEAD tags.

Some engines list the page title in searches so it is important to have a title that is understandable and clearly explains the purpose of your page.

An example of how this works is shown below.

```
<html>
<head>

<meta name="description" content="computer training &
problem solving">
<meta name="keywords" content="lecturer, writing web
pages, computer advice">

<title>david weale's business page
</title>

</head>

<body>make sure you include keywords within the content
of your page, although this is unlikely to be a problem
</body>

</html>
```

Counters

There is a divergence of opinion here, some people want to include a counter to show the viewer how popular the site is. Others consider it vulgar and counter-productive (especially if the counter has a low reading). I guess if you want to know how many hits your page has received then you can use a **hidden** counter.

You can find more information about counters on the Net, one site is:

http://beseen.com/beseen/free/counters.html

Why go on the Internet

Gaining experience

Eventually all businesses will have a presence on the Internet and it will become the main communications medium for both individuals and businesses.

Creating a presence now on the Net and going through the learning curve makes sense, you will gain considerable advantages over your less imaginative competitors.

Research and information

The Net is a worldwide databank or library of information on every conceivable topic and most of the information is free to access or download.

Publicise your products

You can create an on-line catalogue of your products or the services you can supply. You can also publicise your company and the people who work in it.

You could also create an on-line magazine or newsletter; it may be worthwhile to create an interesting (content and visually) newsletter. This could provide information about your organisation and the people in it, contact points and so on.

An on-line presence is cheaper and may be more effective than producing glossy brochures.

Provide customer support

After sales information or technical guides and so on can be provided on your web pages. You may want to include a page of FAQs (frequently asked questions) on your site.

E-mail

Electronic mail is faster, cheaper and more reliable than 'snail mail'. This is useful both to communicate with customers and with your sales force when they are out selling.

You can also build up a database of E-mail addresses from customers and other responses to advertising material and then use this database as a marketing tool.

Cheap and easy

After the initial hardware costs and your subscription to the information provider, your only outlay is the cost of local telephone charges (and staff time).

Keep up to date with software releases

Many software suppliers offer programs for downloading; these may be fixes, beta versions of new software or freebies. There are specific sites dealing in shareware and public domain programs.

Teleworking

You may want to investigate the idea of your employees working from home or you may want to recruit additional or contract staff to work on projects without having to physically accommodate them.

Recruitment

You can recruit from on-line electronic CVs and employee databases, which can be quicker, and more efficient than traditional methods, Reed Employment has a web site as does the PeopleBank.

Glossary

Archie	A program to find on-line material - an older form of retrieval, superseded by the WWW
Backbone	The infrastructure of the internet, data travels from one network to another via the backbone
Bandwidth	How much data can be sent along a connection
Baud rate	Measures the speed of data travelling along communication lines, measures in Kbps (kilobytes per second)
Browser	The program that enables you to view HTML documents (both on-line and off-line)
Dial-up	Connect to the Net
Domain	The address of the host computer
Download	Transfer data from a web site to your computer
E-mail	Electronic mail - you have an e-mail address in a similar way to your home address
FAQ	Frequently asked question, many sites have a list of FAQs so you can learn the basics about the site
Flame	An e-mail (not nice) sent to the originator of a message, it has been known for thousands of people to flame a particular site, jamming the server
FTP	File transfer protocol - a quick way of transferring files from one Net site to another

Gopher	Means 'Go For' - a method of finding the information you require using a menu system - in a sense the antecedent of the WWW but still used today
Home page	The first page for a site (normally Index.htm)
HTML	Hypertext mark-up language - the code in which web pages are written
HTTP	Hypertext transfer protocol (how HTML documents get transferred around the Net)
Hypertext link	A link from one web page to another - normally shown in a different colour from the remainder of the text, it can be a graphic or text
Intranet	An internal (company) internet using the same protocols, it makes accessing company wide data easy and cheap compared with traditional methods (only one copy of documents exist and they are held centrally on the server)
Java	A programming language for internet applications
Modem	Modulator/demodulator - hardware that translates digital data into analogue and back again (so the data can travel the telephone system)
Netiquette	Behave or you will be flamed
Newsgroup	A Usenet discussion group

On-line	Connected to the Net and using the telephone lines, off-line means using Net tools, e.g. browsers without being connected
POP	Point of presence - your telephone access point
Plug-ins	Additional programs for web browsers
Server	The computer which hosts the web site
Snail mail	Traditional physical post systems
Spam	Sending a message to many Usenet newsgroups - normally a breach of Netiquette
Telnet	Allows you to take control of a remote computer - obviously access is restricted to certain public sites
URL	Uniform resource locator - the internet address
Winsock	A Windows file that enables Windows to communicate with the Net servers
WWW	World wide web - the visually interesting part of the Net and the most used.

Index